THE
ALLOTMENT
BOOK

THE ALLOTMENT BOOK

ROB BULLOCK
AND
GILLIE GOULD

ILLUSTRATED BY DICK CLARK

An OPTIMA book

© Rob Bullock and Gillie Gould

First published in 1988 by
Macdonald Optima, a division of
Macdonald & Co. (Publishers) Ltd

A member of Pergamon MCC Publishing Corporation plc

British Library Cataloguing in Publication Data

Gould, Gillian
  The allotment book.
  1. Organic gardening 2. Plants, Edible
  3. Working-men's gardens
  I. Title II. Bullock, Robert
  635   SB453.5

ISBN 0-356-12890-3

Macdonald & Co. (Publishers) Ltd
3rd Floor
Greater London House
Hampstead Road
London NW1 7QX

Photoset in 10pt Century by ⧘ Tek Art Ltd, Croydon, Surrey

Printed and bound in Great Britain by
The Guernsey Press Co. Ltd.,
Guernsey, Channel Islands

CONTENTS

ACKNOWLEDGMENTS

The authors would like to thank Trevor Myers and Annie Blindell for reading the manuscript and offering advice, Rose Ardron for helping with the typing (and support!), Sheffield Co-operative Development Group for the loan of the word-processor, John Button for all his help and encouragement as our editor and friend, local authorities for supplying information, and Ben for his amazing patience.

1.
THE HISTORY OF ALLOTMENTS

The term 'allotment' was first coined to describe parcels of land which were divided up between landowners under the Land Enclosure Acts of the late eighteenth and early nineteenth centuries.

A major consequence of the Enclosure Acts was to deprive the landless poor of the right to common grazing which they had held for centuries. They could no longer keep the cow, pig or flock of geese which in the past had provided their basic needs. They were reduced to a state of abject poverty and forced either to rely on landowners and farmers for occasional work, for which they were paid a pittance, or to seek the support of the parish. One commentator of the day wrote that even the African slaves in the West Indies who were given a cottage and allotment of land on which to grow food had a more tolerable existence than the English farm labourer.

In a very few places labourers were leased small parcels of land (usually no larger than they could work in their spare time), but in general the landowners and farmers were only concerned with maintaining a large, mobile and pitifully paid labour force which was totally dependent on them for subsistence.

The compensation for the loss of common grazing rights of rural labourers remained a contentious issue. While a few members of the governing class campaigned for this compensation, the labourers began to take matters into their own hands, destroying machinery and firing hay ricks and buildings. Attempts to organise trade unions were outlawed, and those found guilty of 'criminal' acts against persons and property were either imprisoned, transported or hung.

Against this backdrop of oppression and civil unrest the allotment movement slowly made ground. By 1833 42 per cent of all parishes in England and Wales were known to have allotment schemes, and by 1850 allotments were recognised as areas of land provided by individuals or public bodies as acts of charity on which the labouring poor might supplement their low income by cultivating fruit and vegetables or stock-keeping in their spare time.

The allotment tenant had to abide by strict rules: to attend church, not to work the land on Sunday, to bring up his family in a decent and orderly manner, or lose his tenancy if convicted of any offence. An article in the *Penny Magazine* in 1845 states that 'the object of making such allotments is moral rather than economic, the cultivation of a few vegetables is a pleasing occupation, and has a tendency to keep a man at home and from the ale house'.

In developing industrial towns such as Birmingham, Coventry and Sheffield, a flourishing allotment system already existed. These allotments, or 'small gardens' as they were known, are shown on maps as early as 1731. They cost as much as a guinea a year to rent and seem to have provided recreation for the middle-class people living nearby, who cultivated them as ornamental and productive gardens. Allotments were introduced into other urban areas from the early nineteenth century onwards to provide labourers (many of whom had been forced by the Enclosure Acts to move into the towns) with an opportunity to supplement their low wages by growing fruit and vegetables.

Between 1850 and 1865 allotments were reappraised. Many authorities, including the Poor Law Commissioners, thought that the provision of allotments should be left to private philanthropy, without intervention by the state. Of 614,800 acres of rural land enclosed between 1845 and 1869, only 2,223 acres were assigned to the poor. In 1876 the Enclosure Commissioners were compelled by Parliament to set aside land for the poor. In one instance this land was mortgaged to finance the building of a workhouse! It was not until 1882 that the trustees of the assigned land were required to let it as allotments.

The 1887 Allotment Act required local authorities to provide allotments for the labouring population if land could not be found privately. Between 1873 and 1895 the number of rural plots rose from 244,268 to 482,901. The Smallholdings and Allotments Act of 1908, which consolidated the existing legislation, is recognised as the basis of the modern allotment system.

Demand for allotments still far exceeded supply. In 1916, in the depths of World War I, the Defence of the Realm Act empowered local authorities to secure as much land as was required for the provision of allotments. Fifty thousand acres of land including parks, playing fields and undeveloped building land were requisitioned for 'wartime plots'. The railway and mining companies also made land available, and an intensive advertising campaign, 'Every man a gardener', encouraged people to take up allotments in an effort to relieve the wartime food crisis. The response to the scheme was overwhelming, especially in towns and cities, and the number of allotments rose from 600,000 to 1.5 million between 1913 and 1918.

The urban allotment holders had more money and leisure time, and considered gardening more as a recreation than did their rural counterparts. There was greater demand for surplus crops in urban areas, and co-operation on large sites and subsidised bulk provision of manure and lime aided the scheme.

Between the two World Wars the number of allotments declined, land requisitioned during World War I was returned to its owners, as the need for industrial and domestic land grew. On the other hand, various acts of Parliament improved security of tenure and made allotments available to any applicant, not just the labouring population.

During the depression of the 1930s, a national scheme known as 'Allotment Gardening for the Unemployed' was set up to provide the unemployed with allotments at low rents with subsidised tools, seeds and fertilisers.

At the beginning of World War II a scheme similar to that of the 1914–1918 war was initiated to cultivate any spare land. It was so successful that by 1945 the 'Dig for Victory' allotments were estimated to be producing 10 per cent of all the food produced in Britain. 'Dig for Victory' was renamed 'Dig for Plenty' in 1947, when the role of allotment gardening in helping to alleviate the post-war austerity of food shortages and rationing was recognised.

Since 1945 the demand for allotments has again steadily declined. The increased availability of a greater variety of cheap vegetables, better living standards, the development of other leisure activities and the demand on land for building have all contributed to this decline.

Under the 1950 Allotment Act, every local authority has an obligation to provide four acres of allotments for each thousand of its population. In reality this has never been achieved, not even in the 'Dig for Victory' and 'Dig for Plenty' campaigns during and after World War II.

On the brighter side, however, some local authorities positively encourage the use of allotments by providing special work teams who carry out maintenance work – clearing old allotments, replacing fencing, and improving access paths and other facilities.

Bristol City Council pioneered the concept of leisure gardens by opening a chalet site in 1970. Each well-fenced plot is provided with a cedarwood chalet, and the tenants are encouraged to cultivate the plots with lawns, herbaceous plants and shrubs as well as vegetables. The site is provided with a good road, car park and toilets. In 1987, Hounslow Borough Council opened a similar site to provide for council tenants who do not have a garden of their own.

Today most of the land used for allotments is owned by local authorities, although it is sometimes leased to organisations and bodies. A small amount of allotment land is owned by the National Coal Board (British Coal), by regional water authorities, and by British Rail and other landowners.

The current growth of interest in health and fitness is making people aware of the possible detrimental effects of the use of chemical pesticides and fertilisers on food crops, and allotments provide the organic gardener with land to grow vegetables and fruit more to her or his liking.

2.
WHERE TO BEGIN

The availability of allotments varies throughout the country. Nearly all local authorities have waiting lists, but these can vary enormously: in Sheffield for instance it generally takes less than a year to get an allotment, while acquiring one in the London Borough of Camden may take at least seven years.

Allotment sites can be found throughout the country. They vary from sites containing hundreds of plots to others with nor more than a dozen; and in terms of facilities there are sites which boast toilets, and some which do not even have a water supply.

It is useful to visit all the allotment sites in your locality before making a choice. If you do not know where the allotments are, your local authority, library, civic information service or citizens' advice bureau will almost certainly be able to help. If it is possible to be placed on the waiting list for an allotment in your area, think carefully about which locations are likely to be the most practical and accessible. One of the most important factors to consider is the distance of the favoured site from your home. This may involve a longer wait for a vacancy on a particularly popular site close at hand, but once such an allotment has been obtained it is more likely to be visited and tended. People who grow vegetables in their back garden do not need to plan journeys and only have to walk the length of their garden path to begin work, while the allotment holder has to organise transport of seedlings, compost material and tools, and the greater the distance involved, the more difficult the problem becomes.

The cost of an allotment varies from region to region. In 1987 for instance the annual rent in Newcastle, Norwich,

Bristol, and Exeter was £17, £15.40, £12, and £10.50
respectively. The rental of allotments has increased over the
years – in Norwich for example it was £2 in 1970, £6 in
1980, and £14 in 1985 – and generally they have greatly
increased in price over the last five years. In 1936,
allotments in Sheffield cost 2d a week, eight shillings and
sixpence a year. In 1987 they cost more than £15 a year, and
this charge increases annually. Some local authorities offer
rent reductions to the unemployed, old age pensioners and
other disadvantaged people.

To most of us, allotment gardening is first and foremost a
hobby, though one that can easily become a preoccupation. It
requires commitment of time and money, and if one of these
commodities is plentiful then the other is very often scarce!

It is important to consider this balance between available
time and money as you think about how you intend to
garden your plot. Once a raised bed or no-dig system has
been established, it should need far less labour than a dig
and hoe system, although a raised bed system needs large
quantities of mulching material to maintain it, much of
which will probably have to be bought.

Making your own equipment – cloches, shed, tools – may
save money but costs dearly in time. Making enough garden
compost to feed the soil will require a continuous regime of
collecting vegetable waste from shops and neighbours,
whereas a trailer-load of manure can be delivered to the plot
with a single 'phone call and a dip into the wallet.

It's impossible to say how much time, in hours per week,
will have to be spent on a new allotment, because it very
much depends on the condition it is in when you take it on.
You could of course spend all day every day 'up the plot', for
there is always something to do.

The financial cost of running an allotment can be divided
into the following categories:

Initial capital cost
The purchase of the basic tools you need to start work. These
should last as long as you do!

Yearly running costs
Money for rent, manure and fertiliser, seeds and plants.
These costs should be easily recouped by the harvest of
vegetables.

Special projects

Once the land is under control and there is time to develop growing methods and a variety of crops, cash may have to be found for materials to construct cloches and frames (and possibly a greenhouse), timber and netting for a fruit cage, special tools, and perennial plants.

Having an idea of what expenses might be involved can help you to be prepared for them when they arise. If the allotment is to be financed from a collective purse it may be a good idea to make all the contributors aware of the costs at the beginning.

Sharing an allotment might be the answer to long waiting lists or lack of spare time. The plot can be physically divided into separate areas where each person is responsible for their part, or the work of the whole allotment can be shared, each partner taking responsibility for the cultivation of particular vegetables. It is very important to agree in advance on the method of gardening and the plan you are going to follow, in order to avoid later disputes and bad feelings. There are many advantages to sharing an allotment: the pleasure of working with a friend, sharing knowledge, skills and learning, not to mention the more practical aspects such as running costs, dividing the work load, and covering during holiday periods. Difficulties may arise through differing levels of effort, commitment and knowledge, and although these may be understood at the beginning they can easily change with time. We have both had some very happy and successful experiences of sharing allotments. Rob's father and uncle shared an allotment for many years – one grew vegetables in his half while the other grew prize chrysanthemums. Another possibility may be to cultivate a neighbour's garden in return for shared produce, assuming the neighbour will not be moving in the forseeable future. This can work well, especially with elderly people who can no longer manage their own gardens themselves but would still like them looked after. A more drastic measure would be to move to a house with a larger garden, or to an area where allotments are more easily available.

If a group of like-minded people want allotments, it may be possible to approach and negotiate with a local authority or other body for a piece of waste land, to be used either temporarily, until the site is developed, or on a permanent basis. This was successfully done in an inner city area of

Birmingham, where a group of unemployed people took over a piece of wasteland and now grow vegetables and keep chickens, goats and rabbits. Birmingham City Council were so impressed that they are now investing money in a new scheme to train 80 long-term unemployed people to grow and market Asian and Caribbean vegetables. This shows what can be done from small beginnings and with a degree of vision.

Some local authorities may not be as far-sighted and co-operative as Birmingham, but with the support of the local Friends of the Earth and Soil Association groups they may be persuaded to act.

Many allotment sites have a local allotment society, which provides a focal point where tenants can meet. The society usually provides a shop or hut where you can buy materials and fertilisers on site and at a cheaper price than in garden centres and shops. They may also run competitions, have discussions, and be involved in annual horticultural shows. The societies are run by volunteers and are always pleased to receive extra help. If there is no society or shop on your site, and once you have settled on your allotment and feel you have time, energy and the support of other gardeners, it may be possible to set one up. The National Society of Allotment and Leisure Gardeners offers support to local groups; it has a library, holds meetings and conferences, and supplies general information on request. It also runs an insurance scheme against loss and damage to equipment from theft and vandalism.

There are several organisations both nationally and locally which promote organic and environmental practices. The Soil Association promotes organic farming on a large scale and discourages the indiscriminate use of persistent pesticides and artificial fertilisers on the land. They run courses on organic farming and husbandry and have a registration scheme for organic farms and smallholdings which can then use the Association's organic produce symbol. They give guidelines and help where needed and inspect the land periodically to ensure that the organic standard is maintained. There are local groups which meet regularly, often having guest speakers as well as organising trips to each other's gardens and places of special interest.

The Henry Doubleday Research Association is a national organisation based near Coventry, whose aim is to encourage methods of gardening that do not use artificial fertilisers and pesticides. They carry out research to investigate and improve organic methods, campaign on issues related to organic gardening, and have set up a seed bank so that members can keep in cultivation some of the old varieties which can no longer legally be sold. The centre near Coventry, called Ryton Garden, has 10 acres of land laid out as demonstration gardens which are open to the public. It displays organic gardening techniques, herb, rose and bee gardens, pest control, compost making, soil fertility displays, and an area of wildlife and conservation. Members receive a quarterly newsletter, a free advice service, and free entrance to the gardens.

Friends of the Earth is a national organisation with many regional groups which research and campaign on environmental issues including organic husbandry, paper recycling, energy conservation and toxic waste disposal. They carried out an enquiry in 1978 into the changing role and economic benefits of allotments.

In some large inner city areas there are city farms where local people, especially children, work together growing vegetables and looking after the livestock. Many of the people involved have had no or very little contact with the countryside, and this is a way of bringing the countryside to the people. City farms are always pleased to have extra help, and thereby you can learn new skills. Some farms run courses on animal husbandry, making compost, and growing plants from seeds.

3.
TOOLS AND EQUIPMENT

Some gardening tools are essential. Spend as much as you can afford on brand new tools to get the best quality possible – they will last you a long time. Visit a wide range of shops to do your market research, and talk to other people before you buy, comparing the different tools and brands on offer. Try the tools for size and weight. Long-handled tools such as spades and forks can be purchased with extra long shafts for tall people. The most expensive tools are made from stainless steel, which prevents rusting, but cheaper tools can be just as long-lasting if they are looked after properly. Remove the soil after use, oil them with a cloth, and keep them in a dry shed to prevent rusting and deterioration. Try not to leave tools out on the plot between visits.

If you cannot afford brand new tools it may be possible to buy old or reconditioned tools from an auction, market stalls, or other gardeners. Some tools may need renovation - sharpening, the straightening of prongs, or new handles. Buying tools in shop sales can be a good way of getting good quality products at a bargain price. Some tools which are not in constant use (shears, scythe, or hosepipe, for example) could possibly be shared with a friend or neighbour, but tools which are in use regularly are difficult to share.

Gardening tools are big business and it is possible to buy countless other tools which supposedly make the job easier, but which are not strictly necessary. With a little time and ingenuity, home-made alternatives can usually be devised.

Many allotment holders have areas to store odd bits of metal and wood, and an unknowing visitor could be forgiven for wondering what use these can have, but the gardener can visualise uses for all manner of materials. I have found many treasures in rubbish skips – pieces of wood to use as stakes, old carpets to cover the compost heap, and window frames for the construction of cold frames.

HAND TOOLS

Both the fork and the spade are in constant use and should be as solid and strong as possible. Check whether the tools feel balanced and comfortable to handle. Run your hand down the length of the handle to check there are no sharp or rough edges. A good rounded handle – preferably 'D' shaped – is usually more comfortable than a 'T' shape. Some handles are covered in plastic which feel warmer to the touch on cold days, but do slip when wet. If you are unhappy about the weight of regular-sized tools, you might find it easier to manage a fork with short tines – called a lady's fork – and a border spade. It is pointless to buy a heavy fork or spade which, when full of soil or manure, is impossible to lift.

The garden fork is used for making and spreading compost, for harvesting vegetables, and for digging. The spade is used for cutting edges, rough digging, making trenches for peas, potatoes and brassicas, and for emptying the compost heap.

You will need a strong hand trowel for transplanting and for filling plant pots; a hand fork is used for thorough weeding.

There are three basic types of hoe – the draw hoe, the Dutch hoe and the push/pull hoe for weeding larger areas. Opinions differ as to which is the better. The draw hoe has a curved neck and a blade roughly at right angles to the handle. Weeds can be removed by chopping them vertically from above. The draw hoe is also useful for drawing out seed furrows and earthing up. The Dutch hoe has a flat blade in line with the handle, and is moved forward to cut weeds below the surface. A few weeds will inevitably be left in the ground to grow again, but with regular attention weeds can be kept under control. The push/pull hoe has a double edged blade, and works on both forward and return strokes.

The rake is used for breaking down and levelling off roughly dug earth. It is also useful for gathering together gardening debris such as weeds and hedge clippings, and firming the soil after seed sowing.

The sprung-tined cultivator is a less commonly used but excellent tool which will break up the soil to a greater depth than a rake. On well cultivated land this tool will do the

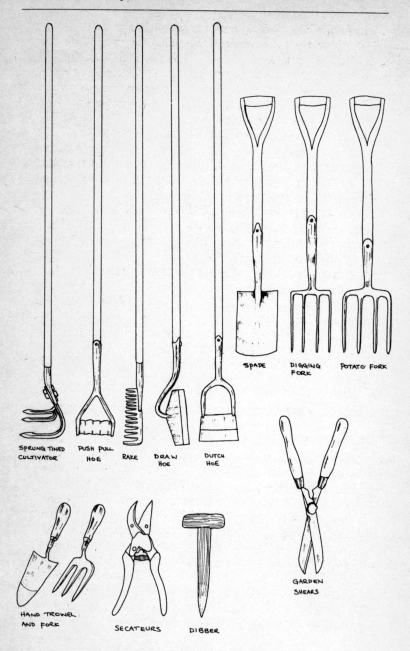

SPADE

DIGGING
FORK

POTATO FORK

SPRUNG TINED
CULTIVATOR

PUSH PULL
HOE

RAKE

DRAW
HOE

DUTCH
HOE

GARDEN
SHEARS

HAND TROWEL
AND FORK

SECATEURS

DIBBER

work of both fork and rake in one operation.

A wheelbarrow is essential for moving heavy or bulky material. Buy one which is sturdily built and suits your size. Before I bought a wheelbarrow I was constantly walking up and down the allotment moving things from one place to another. Now it all fits in the wheelbarrow and can be pushed wherever it is needed.

A watering can is important, especially if there is a greenhouse, when you are sowing seeds and transplanting plants, and for watering in. A hosepipe is useful if the plot has a water supply. When it is not in use keep it rolled up and hung in the shed to prevent deterioration.

If your allotment has a hedge, sooner or later you will need shears to cut it with. Buy shears with a notch in the blade, which can be used for cutting thicker stems. The un-notched ones are for cutting grass only.

Secateurs provide a precise clean cut for pruning fruit bushes and cutting flowers. A dibber may be bought, or home-made by sharpening an old spade or fork handle. It is used for making holes in the ground for planting seeds and seedlings, especially leeks. It is useful to mark it with notches at centimeter or inch divisions.

GARDEN SUNDRIES

A garden line is used for planting vegetables in straight rows to ensure hoeing can take place without damage to the plants. It can be marked in intervals of say 15cm to assist the setting out of plants at their required distances. A rake handle or a length of wood can be marked to act as a ruler, though do not spoil the rake handle (which needs to be smooth for comfortable use) by cutting notches in it. Very soft twine is needed for tying up plants without cutting into the stems. Recycled torn up rags, nylon tights, old bits of bandage or plaited wool scraps can be substituted. Do not use thin hard string as it can cause damage to the plant.

Lollipop sticks or lengths of cut-up washing-up liquid bottles are an alternative to proprietary marker sticks for indicating where seeds have been sown. These should show the date of sowing and the variety used, written with an indelible marker pen.

Proprietary pots are expensive to buy, but every household has plastic containers which can be used instead. Washed yoghurt cartons, margarine tubs and plastic cups will do just as well.

Egg boxes can be filled with seed compost for germinating individual seeds. For more extensive seed sowing, use wooden tomato boxes obtained from greengrocers, or look out for discarded polystyrene packaging – this has the advantage of keeping the soil warm. Large individual pots are expensive, but a 5 litre squash container with the top cut off or a large honey container will contain a growing plant quite adequately. Whatever containers you use, ensure that holes are punched into the base to allow for drainage.

Homemade paper pots can be substituted for peat pots. The seedling roots will grow through the paper so that they can be planted out pot and all. They are easy and cheap to make whatever size you require. The newspaper will eventually rot in the soil.

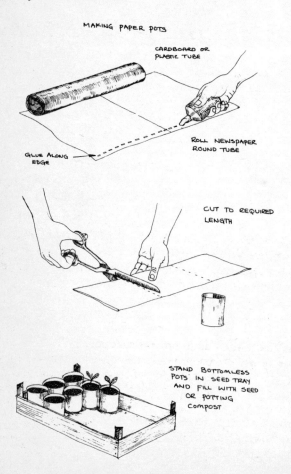

MAKING PAPER POTS

CARDBOARD OR PLASTIC TUBE

ROLL NEWSPAPER ROUND TUBE

GLUE ALONG EDGE

CUT TO REQUIRED LENGTH

STAND BOTTOMLESS POTS IN SEED TRAY AND FILL WITH SEED OR POTTING COMPOST

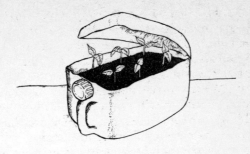

SQUASH CONTAINER   SEED TRAY

UPTURNED JUICE BOTTLE (MINI GREENHOUSE)

Transparent plastic juice bottles cut in half and upturned become mini cloches for delicate seedlings. The thinner types of plastic will disintegrate after one season in the sun, but these can easily be replaced when necessary.

WATER BUTTS

Many allotment sites have no water supply laid on. On those which do, the use of hose pipes is often restricted to filling water butts, and direct watering of the land is prohibited. Collection of rainwater from a shed or greenhouse roof can ease the situation, and if tapwater is available, the siting of water butts around the garden will reduce the labour of carrying watering cans from one end of the plot to the other. Once the soil has achieved a high humus content with the addition of organic matter, watering can be restricted to seed sowing and planting out times, except in extreme drought conditions.

Forty-five-gallon steel drums are easy to obtain and make good water butts. They can be obtained from factories, warehouses, garages or dumps. Check which chemical they contained, and make sure that any remnants have dried or are cleaned off before use. The top of the drum has to be cut off so that you can dip the watering can in. This is best done by cutting round the inside of the rim using a broad-bladed cold chisel or 'bolster' and a 2lb club hammer. This is a very noisy operation, so three-quarters fill the barrel with water before you start, to deaden the noise.

Once the top is removed, a coat of bitumastic paint applied inside and outside the barrel will considerably prolong its useful life. Plastic drums of a similar size, though harder to come by, are more durable, and the top can be removed using a saw.

CLOCHES

A cloche is a moveable shelter made of glass or polythene which is set out over the ground where vegetables are to be grown. The purpose of a cloche is to extend the growing season, providing vegetables out of season when they are expensive to buy.

Cloches are not essential to allotment gardening, but after one or two years' work, when the allotment is more or less under control, there may be time to start experimenting with this method of cultivation.

There are many types of cloche available from garden centres or mail-order advertisements in gardening magazines, but most are expensive. By far the cheapest is the mini polythene tunnel. These can be bought or be home-made. If you decide to make one the materials required are: 500 gauge clear polythene sheeting (available from builders merchants or DIY stores), 5mm thick fence straining wire (available from fencing suppliers, DIY stores and garden centres) and baler twine or strong polythene string.

The wire should be cut into lengths long enough to form a hoop capable of spanning the row you wish to cover, to a maximum width of 60cm, leaving about 25cm at either end to push into the ground. The wire is bent to form a loop at either end at ground level, on to which to tie the string that

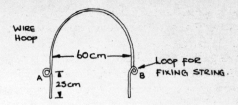

secures the plastic sheeting to the framework. There needs
to be a hoop every metre along the row.

The polythene is cut to width A to B, allowing a little extra
to ensure it touches the ground. Drive a stake into the
ground at either end of the row, and gather the ends of the
polythene in and tie a knot or bind it with string. Spread the
polythene over the hoops and tie it securely to the stakes at
either end. Lastly tie the polythene down on either side of
each hoop, attaching the string to points A and B.

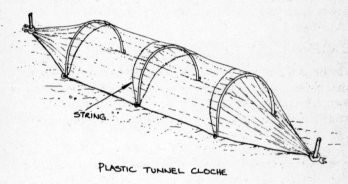

PLASTIC TUNNEL CLOCHE

The polythene may be raised to allow ventilation or to
provide access for weeding and watering.

GREENHOUSES

Most gardeners will eventually want the benefits which a
greenhouse can provide – starting plants from seed, and
growing tender crops which need warmth and protection.

The main difficulty with having a greenhouse on an
allotment is that the crops need constant supervision –
ventilation, watering and heating require daily attention. If
possible, it is best to have the greenhouse in your back
garden or yard.

The fact remains, however, that many people do grow very
worthwhile crops in their allotment greenhouses without

heating or constant supervision. Tomatoes and cucumbers bought from the garden centre or from a neighbour, planted in May and watered once or twice a week, may provide more fruit than you can eat! The ventilation problem can be overcome by fitting automatic ventilator controls.

The siting of greenhouses is dealt with in Chapter 7 – 'Planning the allotment'.

When deciding which greenhouse to buy, shop around carefully – DIY superstores, garden centres, cash-and-carry wholesalers, mail-order advertisements in garden magazines and local newspapers. Even supermarkets stock greenhouses nowadays.

The choice between aluminium and wood is largely a personal one. Both have their good and bad points. The more slender frame sections of the aluminium house exclude less light and the structure should be maintenance free. However, they are more susceptible to storm damage and present more condensation problems than wooden greenhouses, which are warmer but require regular maintenance.

The quality of both aluminium and wooden greenhouses varies enormously in design and quality of material – this is usually reflected in the price. Some suppliers will erect your greenhouse free of charge.

COLD FRAMES

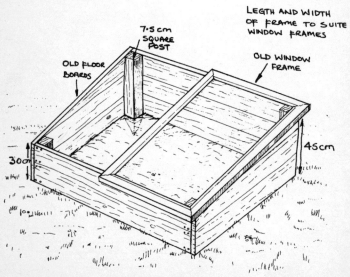

Cold frames were traditionally made with low brick walls and glass roofs, but they may be more usefully constructed with timber sides so that they can be moved each year to fresh ground. the glass roof panels are easily moveable to provide access for cultivation and ventilation.

Cold frames are useful for growing early crops, tender plants in summer, overwintering seedlings, and 'hardening off' between greenhouse and planting out.

An effective cold frame can be made from second-hand timber and old sash windows collected from local builders.

It is important to be able to fix the frames down in some way to avoid possible storm damage. Use a block of wood to prop the windows open. If you make the block 15cm x 7.5cm x 5cm you can vary the amount of ventilation by placing the block on its side or end.

4.
HEALTH AND SAFETY

There are two ailments which could temporarily halt or terminate the gardener's progress – tetanus and back injury.

Tetanus is an illness caused by a bacteria present in soil and manure which can enter the body through the tiniest abrasion, scratch, thorn puncture or cut. Its incubation period is between three weeks and nine months. The disease can cause death within 10 days of onset of symptoms, and it is difficult to diagnose.

Luckily there is a vaccine which can protect you against tetanus. It is administered in three doses at intervals of six weeks, then six months later with booster doses every five years thereafter. These are available from your doctor on the National Health Service.

Back injuries are a much more common problem and much more difficult to guard against. Any continuous hard physical work or lifting of heavy, bulky or awkward loads requires care, practice and an understanding of your capability and physical limitations. Back injuries are most likely to occur when you are unprepared – when the load is unexpectedly heavy or light, stuck or obstructed; when the ground is uneven, slippery or obstructed; or when the load is being lifted awkwardly.

Heavy loads should always be lifted using your leg, not your back muscles.

Check that the load is unobstructed and that the way is clear and safe, and always lift with your back straight and your legs bent. Never try to lift anything which is too heavy or cumbersome for one person. Any load is too heavy if lifting or handling it gives you a feeling of undue effort!

Digging
Digging is probably one of the hardest forms of continuous

physical work which most of us encounter, and it needs to be approached with care.

Never load the spade or fork with more earth than you can easily lift, and work rhythmically, taking frequent rests.

Barrowing

When loading and moving a wheelbarrow, load the barrow towards the front so that most of the load is over the wheel, and fill it centrally so that the load is distributed evenly between the handles. Lift the barrow with your knees bent and your arms and back straight, and make sure that the path is clear and safe. Never load more into a barrow than you can easily lift.

Shifting manure or soil

Placing one hand on the handle and the other on the shaft of the fork or spade as near the load as possible, lift with your knees bent and your back straight. Turn using your feet; never turn by twisting your back. Never load the shovel or fork with more material than you can easily lift.

SHIFTING MANURE OR SOIL

LIFTING HEAVY OBJECT

Lifting

Make sure the load is free and unobstructed. Ensure that you have good hand holds, and if necessary lever the load off the ground and place something underneath it so you can get a good grip on it. Lift it with your knees bent and your feet apart, with the load between your feet or as near to your body as possible, never to one side. If the load is more than you can easily lift, divide it into smaller loads or seek help.

Lifting with a partner
If you need someone's help to move a heavy load, make sure that your helper knows how to lift properly, that you have agreed how you are going to co-operate, and that one of you is taking charge of the operation. If possible enlist the help of someone who is roughly the same height as you.

Watering
A full two-gallon watering can weighs over 6kg. Lift it with your back straight and knees bent. Make sure your pathway is clear.

Garden tools
These can be a hazard if they are improperly stored or left lying around the garden when not in use. Hang your tools up in a shed or lean them tidily against a wall. Rakes and cultivators should be stored with their tines facing the wall.

When you are working with a selection of tools out in the garden, those not in actual use should be made safe. Push forks and spades securely into the ground; do not leave them lying flat on the soil. Rakes and cultivators should be laid on the ground with their tines pushed firmly into the soil. If the upturned tines of a rake are trodden on, the tool handle will fly up and hit the unsuspecting gardener in the face!

A first aid kit is a wise addition to the tools kept in the garden shed; not the sort of kit you carry in the car to save lives on motorways, but a small plastic lunch box containing adhesive plasters, antiseptic ointment, a pair of tweezers for removing thorns and splinters before they have time to become septic, and a gauze or lint pad to use as a compress to stop the bleeding if you are badly cut.

5. SOIL

'We did not inherit this Earth from our parents, but have
been lent it by our children.'   Lester Brown

The advice and information in this book is based on the
principles of organic gardening. Growing organically means
working to provide a natural, fertile environment in which
to grow crops, using fertilisers and pesticides which are of
organic origin based on the natural materials extracted from
living things. An organically rich, fertile soil provides a
home for a multitude of organisms, from earthworms to
fungi and bacteria, which collaborate to produce nutrients in
a form which growing plants can use. One aim of the organic
gardener is to provide the soil conditions in which these
organisms will flourish.

Plants take up nutrients in several ways. The roots of
plants are covered with microscopic hairs known as root
hairs, which only live for a few days; these take up water
and dissolved minerals from the soil. The bacteria in the soil
live off the decomposed root hairs, and convert minerals into
a soluble form which the plants can absorb. The bacteria
need organic matter on which to live, and the plants need
soluble minerals, so the two life forms live in symbiosis.
Certain fungi in the soil find sustenance from root secretions
and convert phosphates from the soil into nutrients, which
the plant can then absorb. Plants also feed through their
leaves, taking in oxygen from the atmosphere and nutrients
applied as a foliar feed.

Chemical fertilisers supply plants with their basic mineral
requirements – nitrogen, potassium and calcium – in a
soluble form which can be taken up by the plants very
quickly; however, they are just as quickly washed out of the
soil by rainfall. They do not supply the soil organisms with
organic matter, and actually suppress fungal and bacterial
activity. Chemical fertilisers do not include trace elements
such as iron, boron, zinc and magnesium which the growing

crops need, and which are found in compost and manure.
The over-application of chemicals can prove very damaging:
fertilisers accidentally applied to leaves will cause scorching
and may prove fatal to the plant.

The organic gardener rejects all but the mildest organic-
based pesticides for several reasons. Pesticides are
indiscriminate, killing not only the pests but also the insects
which prey on them. Destroying the natural balance of
nature can leave the garden even more vulnerable to future
infestations.

Some pesticides are absorbed by the plants and end up on
the dinner table. Most of the vegetables we buy in the
greengrocers have been grown on land treated with
herbicides and chemical fertilisers, and have been sprayed
with insecticides. On a routine check of salad vegetables in
1985, the Environmental Health Laboratory found one batch
of greenhouse-grown lettuce which had been sprayed 46
times with 10 different chemicals!

If you are going to put a lot of effort into growing your
own vegetables, you may as well aim for the best possible
quality. This means organically-grown food containing no
chemical residues. We all have a responsibility to preserve
and improve our environment, and by growing plants
organically the gardener has an opportunity to fulfil this
obligation.

SOIL FERTILITY

Maintaining and improving soil fertility is achieved by
adding organic matter to the soil in the form of well-rotted
manure and garden compost, either dug in or applied on the
surface in the autumn. By spring when most of the vegetable
crops are sown, the manure will have rotted down well, and
the soil will have a good structure, a 'fine tilth' as gardeners
say.

Manure and compost keep the soil open and porous,
creating passages for air to enter and for water to drain
away. They provide plant nutrients, and the bacteria which
are present convert complex nitrogen compounds to nitrites
which can be taken up by the plant. They are also an
important source of humus. Humus is the name given to
vegetable material in its intermediate stage between raw
organic matter and plant food. It is the mass of fibres left
after the softer parts of vegetable material have rotted away.

With continuous cultivation the humus in the soil is used up
and organic matter must be continuously applied to replace
it.

Humus is important in the soil, as it:

- darkens the soil so that it warms up quickly in spring
  and holds the heat for a longer time than impoverished
  soil.
- acts like a sponge and helps to retain moisture in the
  soil.
- supplies plant foods as it decomposes. The acids and
  gases given off during this process help to free and
  preserve other plant foods which would otherwise be lost.
- acts as a buffer, preventing great changes of acidity,
  alkalinity and salinity in the soil.
- improves the soil structure, binding single grain
  particles in sandy soils to form crumbs, and breaking
  down heavy clay soils.

It is easy to make a quick check on the quality of the crumb
structure of your soil. Take a handful of soil half an hour
after it has rained, squeeze it, and open your hand and look
at the structure of the soil. If one large mass forms which
sticks to your fingers, then it will flood in winter and cake
into blocks in the summer. If it powders between your
fingers then it is poor sandy soil which will not retain water.
Good soil is deep in colour – black, dark brown, or red in
sandstone country. It should hold the print of your palm for
about a minute and then unfold into decent sized crumbs
with plenty of fibrous matter in them.

The best garden soils are about 30cm deep, but many
gardens have soil no deeper than 20cm. Below this top layer
is the subsoil. This may look similar to the topsoil but does
not contain as many living bacteria or as much organic
matter. The subsoil affects the drainage: gravel or sand
subsoils tend to drain too quickly, while clay subsoils
prevent drainage causing the surface to become waterlogged.

Soil is a complex mixture of many constituents. This
mixture can vary from area to area, and even within one
allotment! The mineral part of soil is made up of particles
which are classified according to their size: sands, silts, and
clays. Most soils in Britain are made up of a mixture of
these different types of particle, a mixture known as loams,
though the soil will take on the characteristics and
peculiarities of whichever type of particle is dominant.

Sandy soil

A sandy soil has large particles which do not stick together
easily to form crumbs. The spaces between the particles are
large, so the soil contains plenty of air and drains easily,
allowing it to heat up quickly in the spring but depleting it
of nutrients. Sandy soils need plenty of humus to bind the
particles together, slowing down the drainage while
retaining and adding nutrients. One advantage of sandy soil
is that it can be worked at most times of the year.

Clay soil

Clay soils have microscopic particles which have a tendency
to stick together. The soil feels like putty, smooth and silky
to the touch. A pure clay is extremely sticky, with few air
spaces; water cannot drain through it easily. These soils are
wet and difficult to cultivate during rainy periods and
during the winter and are slow to dry out and warm up in
spring. If dug when wet they will tend to 'pan' into dry
impenetrable lumps which are difficult to work. Dig clay
soils in the autumn and leave them so that the frost and
wind can break them down, making them easier to work in
the spring. Organic matter will improve drainage and the
crumb structure.

Loamy soil

This is an ideal blend of sand and clay, the sand keeping the
soil open, the clay retaining the moisture and nutrients –
the gardeners dream!

Calcareous or chalky soils

These soils which often overlie chalk or limestone, are
deficient in plant food and rather shallow in depth. They
lack humus, so lots of organic matter should be incorporated
into the soil. When wet the soil is sticky, but in dry periods
it does not retain moisture. Chalk can cause stunted growth
and a yellowing of leaves known as chlorosis. It does not
usually need lime, and club root disease, the bane of the
brassica family, hardly ever occurs on chalk soils.

Peaty soil

Peat is formed over thousands of years by the decay of
vegetable matter in waterlogged conditions; consequently,
peaty soils contain as much as 20 per cent humus but are
very 'sour' or acidic. Once peaty soils are well worked and

lime is added to neutralise the acidity, they provide a good growing medium.

SOIL ACIDITY

Soil fertility is greatly affected by its acidity or alkalinity, which can be scientifically measured. This acid/alkaline balance, which is known as the pH of the soil, is measured on a scale of pH0–14; pH1 being most acid and pH7 being neutral. A difference of one point on the scale indicates a 10-fold increase or decrease in acidity or alkalinity.

Garden soils are usually acidic, around pH5–6. In towns, industrial pollution often increases soil acidity to pH4. Chalk soils are likely to be pH7 or over. In horticulture, plant growth will only occur between pH3.5 and pH8, although the optimum level for cultivation is pH6.5–7. Little will grow on very acid soils – only heather and bracken will grow on peat hillsides, both being acid-loving plants.

The pH of the soil is very important as it affects the quantity, type and distribution of micro-organisms in the soil, which in turn control the availability of mineral nutrients required by the plants. Most organic materials that are added to the soil are acidic, and their decomposition

Ph

	4	5	6	7	8

NITROGEN

PHOSPHORUS

POTASH

CALCIUM

MAGNESIUM

IRON

MANGANESE

BORON

EFFECTS OF Ph VALUE ON NUTRIENT UPTAKE

DENOTES Ph RANGE AT WHICH NUTRIENTS ARE AVAILABLE

by micro-organisms further increases this acidity. As the soil becomes more acid, nitrogen, phosphorus, and potassium become less available to the plant, and calcium totally unavailable. However, the trace elements, iron, aluminium, and manganese become readily available and can cause toxicity symptoms.

When the soil increases in alkalinity, over pH7, nutrients such as nitrogen, phosphorus, and potassium become totally unavailable. Therefore, for optimum plant development the soil ideally needs to be within the narrow range of pH 6.5–7.

Small differences in the soil pH affect the growth of plants. Some will be retarded in growth while others will flourish, potatoes prefer an acid soil (pH4.5–5) while brassicas prefer an alkaline soil (pH7.3–7.5). This is one reason why adding manure and lime in a specific sequence in the crop rotation is important.

Testing the pH of your soil
To find out the pH of your soil, a simple test can be carried out. Collect three or four samples of soil from different parts of the garden and place each in a small jar. Add 20cc of distilled water and shake the samples vigorously. Leave them to separate into mud and liquid. Dip a piece of litmus paper in each sample of liquid (this can be bought from any chemist which stocks wine-making apparatus) and match it up to the numbered coloured chart which comes with the litmus paper. This will indicate the pH of the soil. You can buy a pH meter which gives you a direct reading on a scale, but these are relatively expensive for the number of occasions you might use one throughout the year. There are also proprietary kits available from garden centres which will determine the pH; some also allow you to check nitrogen, phosphorus and potassium levels as well.

If the soil is found to be alkaline, adding garden compost and manure will reduce the alkalinity. Usually the soil is too acidic, and this can be corrected by using calcium. Garden lime (hydrated lime) can be used to neutralise soil acidity, but this should be used with care, since it is very easy to take the pH above 7. It is safer to use ground limestone (calcium carbonate), magnesium limestone (dolomite) or calcified seaweed, which will not take the pH above 7 if applied at a rate of 225g per square metre (alternatively use garden lime at no more than 60g per square metre). Lime should never be applied to the soil at the same time as animal manure as they will react together chemically, the nitrogen in the manure being converted to ammonia gas and lost.

WHEN AND HOW TO DIG

Soil should not be dug when it is very wet or very dry, as this will damage the soil structure as well as being very hard work.

Double digging
Many gardeners recommend double digging the land if it has not been cultivated for several years, in order to remove deep rooted perennial weeds and to ensure good drainage and aeration of the soil. Double digging means that the soil is dug two 'spits' or spade-lengths deep.

How to double dig
Mark out a strip of land about 60cm wide across the bed which is to be dug.
1. Take out the top spit of soil to form a trench, and barrow the soil to the other end of the bed.
2. Using a fork, loosen the soil of the lower spit. Some gardeners recommend that manure, rotted compost, annual weeds or turf be added to this trench.
3. Dig out the next top spit, placing the soil in the first trench.
4. Loosen the soil of the lower spit. Repeat this process to the end of the bed, filling the last trench with the soil from the wheelbarrow.

Single digging
If the soil has been double dug once, single digging should be adequate. This consists of turning the land over to one spit depth, incorporating manure and removing all perennial weed roots as you go.

Other gardeners think that double digging is not worth the considerable effort it entails, while the devotees of the no-dig system contend that any form of digging is detrimental to soil structure and should be avoided wherever possible.

No-digging method
In the no-digging method the compost or manure is laid on the surface of the soil and taken down into the soil by the

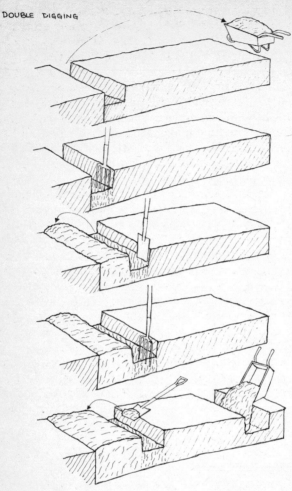

DOUBLE DIGGING

worms who thus do the work for us. At Arkley Manor in
Barnet, Hertfordshire, the no-digging method has been used
very successfully for the past 27 years. The gardens are very
productive, growing flowers, shrubs, fruit and vegetables.
From controlled experiments at Arkley it appears that
placing rotted organic matter on the surface is more
beneficial and produces better crops than digging manure
into the soil. The worms seem to benefit too. They are
constantly working vertically up and down through the soil,
incorporating the organic matter into it, and producing
perfect channels for air and moisture to percolate. Worms
process enormous quantities of soil and organic matter,

mixing it together and adding gum and lime as it passes through their stomachs. When worms die their protein-rich bodies decay, and nitrogen is returned to the soil. If manure or compost is buried in the soil it is excluded from the oxygen and soil bacteria which are necessary to break it down into plant nutrients. Breakdown will occur but much more slowly, and nutrients will not become available to the plants until the following year when the soil is dug again. The no-digging method makes food available to the plants where they can use it most efficiently, within the top 10cm of soil. By placing manure or compost on the surface it is available for plant use almost immediately.

Sedge peat can be used on the surface instead of compost if calcified seaweed at 100g per square metre is added. Sedge peat is preferable to other peat as it contains over 100kg of immediately available humus per tonne, in comparison to 20kg with sphagnum peats. Sedge peat is less acid than sphagnum peat (pH5.5 compared with pH3.8) so there is no danger in using it on the surface.

The no-digging method can be incorporated into a mulching system, or manure can be applied in the autumn. In spring the soil can be raked over before sowing and planting.

The no-digging method can be employed on meadow, or very weedy land by first mulching it as described later in this chapter. The soil need never be dug, thus saving both your time and your back!

Raised beds
In this system the garden is divided by narrow paths into beds 1.2–1.5 metres wide, enabling the beds to be worked without treading on them. The beds are deeply dug to remove weeds, organic matter is added, and some soil is removed from the paths and added to the bed. Unlike the row method of cultivation where all the ground is manured yet some is not cultivated, in raised bed cultivation you only feed the growing areas. Crops can be grown closer together than conventional spacing, giving higher yields for the space used. This method requires less maintenance as only the bed areas need attention, and many of the weeds are smothered by the closely spaced crops. The soil structure is more open as the beds are not walked on, and as they are raised, drainage is improved. The soil also tends to warm up earlier in the spring so that crops can make an earlier start.

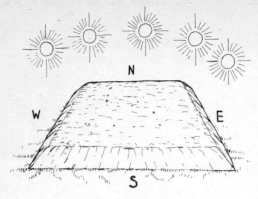

RAISED BED – DIRECTION

MULCHING

Mulching is a technique used especially in 'no-dig' systems, and involves keeping the ground covered with a layer of organic material. Peat, lawn mowings, garden compost, manure, rotted straw, mushroom compost, wilted comfrey, bracken, spent hops, newspaper, cardboard, seaweed and leafmould can all be used as mulches. All these materials will eventually decompose into the soil.

Mulching the soil has several advantages:

- it controls weeds.
- it retains the moisture in the soil by preventing evaporation.
- it stabilises the temperature of the soil and the air just above it, keeping the soil cool in summer and warm in winter.
- it helps the soil structure by encouraging worm activity.
- it helps keep crops clean and prevents mould infestations.
- it adds nutrients to the soil and protects light soils from winter weathering and rain.

Mulches can be applied to uncultivated and cultivated soil at almost any time of the year except during frosty winter weather or when the soil is very dry.

Mulching is an ideal way of bringing a new piece of land to a workable and fertile condition, and it is best to mulch in spring when the weeds are trying to grow. If the weeds already have a foothold on the land they can be cut with a scythe and left on the ground. Annual weeds will be smothered by applying a mulch 10cm thick, but perennial

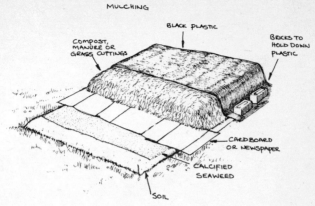

MULCHING

BLACK PLASTIC

COMPOST, MANURE OR GRASS CUTTINGS

BRICKS TO HOLD DOWN PLASTIC

CARDBOARD OR NEWSPAPER

CALCIFIED SEAWEED

SOIL

weeds will need to be further suppressed by applying a material which will exclude light completely, eventually exhausting their root systems. Suitable mulches for this are black plastic sheeting, old carpets, flattened cardboard boxes, or several thicknesses of newspaper. All these must be held down with bricks, planks of wood or soil around the edges to stop the wind blowing them about.

Previously uncultivated ground can be brought into use within one season using an organic mulch and black plastic. The organic mulch will add nutrients to the soil while the black plastic will smother the weeds and maintain a warm environment for the decaying process.

The ground is first treated with calcified seaweed to balance the pH at 250g per square metre. Opened-out plain cardboard boxes or several sheets of newspaper (but not shiny paper or colour supplements) are then laid which suppress the weeds, followed by 8–10cm of compost which increases the humus content and fertility of the soil. This in turn is all covered with black plastic sheeting and weighted down. The plastic further prevents weed growth and loss of nutrients.

If you use this method to clear land which is badly infested with perennial weeds, it is best to leave it for a year before cultivation. If the land is in better condition it is not necessary to wait a whole season before growing crops on it. Vigorous vegetables such as courgettes, marrows, and potatoes can be planted through slits cut in the black plastic, although the crop yield may be low. If vegetables are grown by this method, watering may become a problem as rain cannot penetrate through the plastic, although water loss by evaporation of the soil is minimised too. On an allotment with lots of weeds it is possible just to cover the land with black plastic if you do not have enough compost – it will still kill the weeds.

On an established allotment, black plastic (with or without a mulch) can be laid on the soil through the winter, preventing leaching of nutrients, encouraging the soil to warm up, and aiding plant growth and the establishment of roots. The plastic should be removed prior to planting.

Mulching is also useful in well-established gardens to enrich the land, suppress annual weeds, and help retain moisture. The mulch should either be applied as described above, or used just to surround the growing plants. It should be at least 5cm thick, and as it is taken into the soil it may need to be replenished later in the season. A grass clipping mulch should be no more than 1.5cm thick. For information about sowing and transplanting plants into mulched ground see pages 70 and 72.

Different mulches are suitable for different purposes:

Mulches

Mulch	Properties	Example of use
Compost	Provides nutrients; too precious to be used for weed control.	Vegetable crops with a long growing period, e.g. brassicas
Well-rotted manure	Provides nutrients; lasts longer if composted first. If used fresh it will burn the plants.	Heavy feeders, e.g. blackcurrants and roses
Straw	Partially rotted straw is preferable. It may contain chemical weed killers (leave out over winter first). Lasts longer than hay.	Keeps fruit clean, e.g. strawberries and marrows
Hay	Good insulator. Can introduce annual weed seeds.	Around fruit trees and bushes
Leafmould	Provides some nutrients, but they are released very slowly.	Use anywhere
Peat	Slow to decompose.	Acid-loving plants
Sedge peat	Provides immediately available humus.	Use with calcified seaweed anywhere
Newspaper-cardboard	Useful under other biodegradable mulches to improve weed control.	Around fruit bushes and perennial vegetables
Lawn-mowings	Ensure mowings haven't been recently sprayed with herbicides. Only short term weed control. Supplies nutrients, but of little benefit to the soil structure.	Use anywhere; top up for hay or straw mulches

6.
ORGANIC FERTILISERS

Plants are constantly removing nutrients from the soil.
These need to be replenished in order to maintain a healthy,
fertile soil. The best way of doing this is by the application
of well-rotted manure and garden compost, both of which
provide humus as well as balanced plant foods. If the soil is
fed in the right way and kept in good condition the
vegetables we grow, cook and eat will be rich in vitamins
and minerals.

Garden compost can be made from garden and vegetable
waste, but there is a continual problem of obtaining enough
waste to make sufficient compost for our garden's needs.
This can be supplemented by buying in farmyard manure
from farms if the allotment is close to the countryside, or
horse manure from the ever-increasing number of riding
stables springing up around our cities.

Different animal manures contain varying proportions of
elements – nitrogen, phosphorus, and potassium (see chart
below) – as well as useful proteins, natural hormones,
sugars, vitamins, bacteria, and humus, all of them vital for
healthy plants and soils.

Type of manure	nitrogen (%)	phosphorus (%)	potassium (%)
Chicken	1.5	1	0.5
Cow	0.7	0.3	0.9
Farmyard manure	0.6	0.2	0.5
Horse	0.7	0.3	0.6
Pigeon	5	2.4	2.3
Sheep	0.7	0.3	0.9

Fresh unrotted manure must never be added to the soil, as it
will rob the soil of nitrogen, causing the plants to be starved of

this vital element. The roots and stems of the plants can be scorched, and nitrogen starvation may help weeds and fungi spread to the soil. Horse or farmyard manure should be placed in a heap. If the heap is stacked too loosely and gets too dry it will be infected by the firefang fungus, the white threads of which spready rapidly, reducing manure to a dusty-looking mass, so that much of its nitrogen and humus is wasted. When a heap is made, exclude as much air as possible. The heap should be covered with plastic – weighted down at the edges – to stop nutrients from leaching out and nitrogen gas from escaping. Poultry manure is much stronger than horse or farmyard manure and can either be composted separately, with the addition of straw, or used as an activator in the garden compost heap.

Pigeon manure is about the best compost activator there is, and should only be applied to the compost. It should never be used raw as it is too rich in nitrogen.

GARDEN COMPOST

Vegetable and garden waste is converted into garden compost by the action of bacteria. Creating the best conditions for these bacteria is both an art and a science. Compost takes time to make but is well worth the effort involved: in time all your raw vegetable waste will be transformed into a lovely blackish-brown, moist, crumbly compost. Garden compost is best made in two stages, the first requiring oxygen, the second without oxygen. In the first stage air, heat and moisture are needed for the decomposition of the vegetable waste. Plenty of air should be available to enable the aerobic bacteria and fungi to thrive. The bacteria also need moisture, though if the heap is too wet it will prevent good aeration and encourage outrefaction. In this first part of the process heat is generated, and the compost can reach temperatures as high as 82°C within the first few weeks, which encourages the bacteria to multiply and sterilises any weeds and seeds that are present. Turning the heap after 10 days further aerates it, encouraging bacterial activity and thoroughly mixing the heap.

In the second stage the heap is left for several months so that the process of making good quality compost can be completed. This is carried out by anaerobic bacteria and worms, and the heap requires no further turning.

Never add diseased plant material, hard wood prunings or

any artificial products to your compost. Do not add perennial weed roots unless you are sure that the heap will heat up sufficiently to decompose them. When adding vegetable roots or weeds first remove as much soil from them as possible, as it prevents the heap from heating up. If the heap fails to heat up, one of the following signs may indicate that all is not well with your compost heap:

- if woodlice are present the heap is too dry, and water should be added.
- if the heap is decomposing very slowly or not at all, adding urine should help. Urine is a very useful activator, and should start the decomposition process.
- a noxious smell indicates either that the heap is too wet, or that there is not enough oxygen present in the first stage, thus encouraging anaerobic bacteria at the expense of aerobic ones. By turning the heap and adding newspaper or some dry grass clippings, you will absorb the excess moisture so the aerobic bacteria can thrive again.

The compost heap is best made in one operation rather than by adding waste gradually. This can be difficult as household vegetable waste is only obtained in relatively small quantities at any one time. Store all waste until you have sufficient material to make the heap in one operation.

MAKING THE HEAP

Compost can be made in several ways but it should always be made on earth rather than on concrete, to allow worms access to it. Compost is made more quickly in spring and summer than in the winter.

The unsupported compost heap

A network of branches and twigs is first laid on the ground to allow air into the heap. Layers of different materials are then built up to form a heap. The first layer should be partially rotted compost from another heap, or vegetable or garden waste about 22cm thick. The second layer consists of 5–7cm of manure or compost, and a sprinkling of activator – either fish or seaweed meal. This is followed by a further 22cm of organic waste. The fourth layer has an application of sufficient lime or calcified seaweed to whiten the previous layer. This sequence is repeated until the heap is about 1.2 metres high, and water should be added if the waste matter

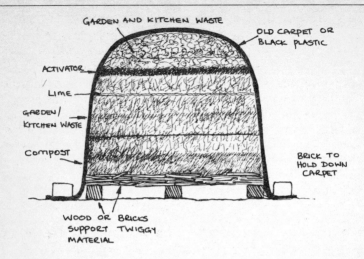

GARDEN AND KITCHEN WASTE

OLD CARPET OR BLACK PLASTIC

ACTIVATOR

LIME

GARDEN/ KITCHEN WASTE

COMPOST

BRICK TO HOLD DOWN CARPET

WOOD OR BRICKS SUPPORT TWIGGY MATERIAL

is dry. The heap should be covered with old carpets and black plastic to retain the heat and moisture. The heap needs turning after two to three weeks to aerate and thoroughly mix it. Using this method it will take six to nine months before the compost is ready for use.

The New Zealand bin

A bin can be made from pieces of old wood. You can either have it fixed in one position, or moveable. The advantage of a collapsible bin is that it can be moved around the growing bed to enrich the soil beneath the rotting compost. The compost is made in the same way as in the unsupported heap, but when it is turned after two to three weeks the heap is either put into an adjacent bin or removed and then replaced.

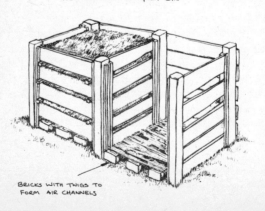

NEW ZEALAND COMPOST BIN

BRICKS WITH TWIGS TO FORM AIR CHANNELS

The plastic bin

A method which is becoming increasingly popular is a bottomless cylindrical plastic bin. Fork over the earth where the bin is to go, and when it is in place fill it in one operation with alternate layers of newspaper (which helps to absorb the excess liquid which is produced), and waste vegetable matter and weeds. After seven to 10 days remove the bin and place it next to the semi-rotted heap. Add more newspaper at the bottom and put the rotted material back. Do not add fresh material at this stage. Leave if for a further 10 days.

To finish off the process the rotted material can be transferred to a New Zealand bin and left for several months while the anaerobic bacteria and worms finish the process.

These plastic bins are relatively expensive to buy, and similar results can be achieved by making small piles of vegetable waste in a similar way and covering them with black polythene sheeting. The advantage of this is that small quantities of compost can be made frequently, which suits the organic offerings of most households.

LEAFMOULD

Leafmould is a valuable source of humus for the soil, although most of the nutrients have been absorbed back into the tree before the leaves fall. There is some danger of lead pollution from leaves, but we only absorb 15 per cent of ingested lead from what we eat, compared with 70 per cent from the atmosphere, so using leafmould in the garden is not a real problem – though it is best to avoid leaves from near busy roads. Leafmould is made in a different way from vegetable compost; since leaves are decomposed by anaerobic bacteria, the process takes about two years, heat is not generated, and it does not require oxygen, activator or lime. Drive four stakes into the ground, and secure wire netting to them to form a cage. This enclosure should be filled with leaves, treading them firmly down every 15cm and watering them if they are very dry. After a year the stakes and netting can be removed and used for the next autumn's leaves – the first stack of leaves should by then be sufficiently firm to stay put. After two years this stack will be about half its original size, and the leaves will have decayed sufficiently to be used as a mulch in the autumn on vegetable and flower beds. Some local authorities will deliver leaves to allotment sites.

LEAFMOULD HEAP

Providing enough compost for the vegetable garden is an impossible task, and it will need to be supplemented by buying in manure or sedge peat, and by growing green manures.

GREEN MANURING

Green manures are leafy crops what are grown either to be dug in, or cut and used for mulching or compost. They can be thought of as making compost *in situ* – adding humus to the soil and improving aeration and drainage. Green manures can be grown in summer or winter, whenever there is spare land on the allotment, though in winter, when most of the soil is bare and unproductive, green manuring is an ideal way of using land. If your soil is left bare, nutrients will be washed away and nitrogen will be given off into the air as ammonia. By growing a green manure crop, the nitrogen will be taken up by the plants and held in an organic form, which will be passed back to the soil when they rot, making nitrogen available for the next crop. Green manure crops also suppress annual weeds. Manure crops should be dug in or scythed down just before they flower, as the plant structure then becomes too tough to be useful.

Green manure can be divided into two groups: leguminous crops which build up nitrogenous nodules on their roots (lupins, clover, vetches, field peas and winter tares), and non-leguminous crops (mustard, rye, rape oats and grass).

The manure crops you grow should be a mixture of leguminous and non-leguminous plants, as the soil will receive nitrogen from one and lots of humus-forming material from the other. For light sandy and gravel soils, lupins and mustard are good together. For clay soils, rye grass and clover or oats and vetches are good combinations.

Winter tares and Hungarian rye should be sown in the autumn. Alfalfa can be used if sown in the late summer, and mustard will survive in mild areas through the winter, even though strictly speaking it is a summer crop.

CULTIVATION OF GREEN MANURES

Green manure seeds can be obtained from farm seed merchants or from the Henry Doubleday Research Association, and sown on any land which will otherwise be bare for eight weeks or more. Lightly fork over the land once the previous crop has been cleared, rake it to produce a reasonable seed bed, and either sow the seeds broadcast or in rows. Hoe them off or dig them in before the foliage and stems become coarse.

Annual lupins – bitter blue
These nitrogen-fixing legumes are sown from April to August, singly 15cm apart in rows 30cm apart and 2.5cm deep. The crop is ready to dig in when the flower stems appear, or may be left to mature to produce seed for the next year's crop. The foliage is then cut off at ground level and composted, leaving the roots to enrich the soil. Brassicas can then be planted without digging, to benefit from the firm ground and the nitrogen supplied by the lupins.

Winter tares
This is another leguminous crop which is sown in September and October, 7cm apart in rows 15cm apart and 13cm deep. The crop is hoed off or dug in the spring when the flower buds show.

Clover – 'late red'
Another legume, which should be sown broadcast at a rate of 45g per 10 square metres, from August to October. It may be mixed and sown with winter grazing rye, to hoe off or dig in the following spring. Brussels sprouts and sprouting broccoli may be undersown with clover in the autumn and cleared when the brassicas are finished.

Grazing rye

This useful winter crop is sown broadcast and raked in at a
rate of 45g per square metre from August to early October.
The crop is dug in when it is no more than 60cm high in the
spring. Do not allow the stems to become too coarse or they
will rob the soil of nitrogen as they decompose. The foliage
may be cut for compost two or three times before finally
digging in the mass of roots.

Mustard

This summer crop is a member of the cabbage family, and
shares Club Root disease with them. It is best not to use it if
Club Root is a problem on your land. In any case, grow it
only infrequently and neither immediately before or after
the brassica rotation. It is, however, a very quick crop to
mature and is an effective cure for wireworm.

Scatter the seed at a rate of 30g per square metre, raking
it in, between April and July. Dig it in while the growth is
still sappy and the flower buds just beginning to show, which
may be in as little as eight weeks from sowing.

Sunflowers

These make excellent compost material and produce a great
bulk of weed-suppressing foliage. Leave them to grow until
they are 1.2 metres high, but before flowering pull them out,
shake off as much soil from the roots as possible and use
them on the compost heap. Several sowings a year can be
made of the striped seeds, which can be bought from pet
shops where they are sold as parrot food.

Comfrey

The leaves of perennial comfrey can be used as a green
manure, but the plants should remain in a permanent bed.
Comfrey provides three to four cuts of foliage a year, which
is rich in nitrogen and potassium. Its deep root system
extracts minerals from the subsoil. Comfrey can be used in
the garden in many ways.

The cut leaves, left to wilt for a day, can be used either as
a mulch or added to the compost heap.

The leaves can also be added to water in a container to
make a comfrey liquid, at a rate of about 1kg of leaf and
stem to every 13 litres of water. The mixture is left for three
to four weeks to decompose and is then ready for use. While
this mixture is fermenting it is unfortunately extremely
smelly, so try to ensure that the container lid is securely sealed.

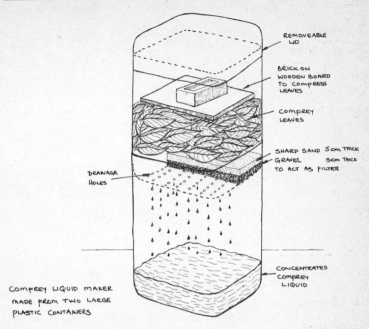

REMOVEABLE LID

BRICK ON WOODEN BOARD TO COMPRESS LEAVES

COMFREY LEAVES

SHARP SAND 5cm THICK
GRAVEL 5cm THICK
TO ACT AS FILTER

DRAINAGE HOLES

CONCENTRATED COMFREY LIQUID

COMFREY LIQUID MAKER MADE FROM TWO LARGE PLASTIC CONTAINERS

Concentrated comfrey liquid can also be made by placing the comfrey leaves and stalks into a container with a lid and a small hole in the bottom. Put a weighted board on top of the comfrey leaves; as the leaves ferment, the juice drips into another container below the hole. New comfrey leaves are added as required. Nettles can also be added to further enrich the mixture. At the end of the growing season the sludge in the container can be added to the compost heap. Before using it the liquid should be diluted to one part comfrey to 30 parts water. The liquid can be used as a foliar feed on plants and vegetables, or as a high potash liquid feed for greenhouse tomatoes, applied weekly.

The best variety of comfrey to grow is Bocking No 14, which is available as offsets from Henry Doubleday Research Association. Many organic gardeners grow this crop and will probably be happy to supply you with roots with which to start your bed.

Comfrey will thrive for many years in one place so the bed, which should be situated in a sunny position, should be completely clear of perennial weeds. Dig in plenty of manure; the plants are tolerant of fresh manure and they will even accept fresh pigeon or poultry manure which is too strong for other crops.

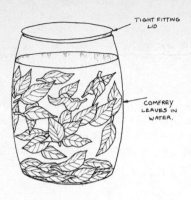

TIGHT FITTING LID

COMFREY LEAVES IN WATER.

READY TO USE LIQUID MANURE.

Plant the root offsets at any time except mid-winter, with the growing point about 5cm below soil level, spacing them 60cm apart either way. Allow the plants to grow without cutting the foliage for the first year. Each spring, fork over the land to remove weeds, and incorporate any manure you have spare. Cut the foliage off about 5cm above ground level when the flower buds appear, using the harvest for making compost, liquid manure, or as instant compost or mulch. If you have to move the comfrey bed for some reason, cut the roots off 5cm below ground level to provide offsets for a new bed, and sprinkle the exposed roots – which go down one or two metres into the subsoil – with ammonium sulphamate or other weed killer, as this is the only way to kill them off.

OTHER ORGANIC FERTILISERS

Sometimes plants will need an extra boost, as well as the food they already receive, either to encourage the general health of the plant, or to encourage fruiting and ripening. This can be provided by various organic fertilisers you can buy, which are rich in specific elements. They are mostly relatively expensive.

Bone meal
This slow acting fertiliser provides the richest supply of phosphorus. It is best applied in the autumn at a rate of 225g per square metre, and is especially useful in the preparation of soft fruit beds because of its long lasting qualities.

Dried blood
This is best used as a tonic for growing plants, applied at a rate of 25g per square metre. It is a very fast acting, high nitrogen fertiliser.

Fish blood and bone meal
This is used as a general fertiliser worked into the soil surface in the spring at a rate of 110g per square metre. It supplies readily available nitrogen for early plant growth and an enduring supply of phosphates for good root development.

Hoof and horn meal
A slow acting supplier of nitrogen, hoof and horn is applied at a rate of 110g per square metre. Combined with bone meal it is useful in the preparation of soft fruit beds.

Seaweed
Seaweed is rich in many trace elements which are difficult to obtain from other sources. It encourages bacterial activity within the soil, releases locked up minerals, improves soil structure, and helps develop a good root system. Seaweed comes in several forms:

Fresh seaweed
Fresh seaweed must be washed to remove the salt. It can then be applied directly to the soil as a mulch, and covered with a layer of grass cuttings, straw or compost to prevent dessication. If the seaweed is to be added to the compost heap, it must dry out for two days in order to lose a large proportion of the water. Seaweed is high in potash and is ideal as a fertiliser for tomatoes. Reports and investigations carried out into radioactivity and other pollution found along much of Britain's coastline has led to reservations about collecting seaweed from around the coastline, so be wary of using contaminated seaweed.

Calcified seaweed
This is collected from the seabed off Brittany and the Cornish coasts. It has a high calcium and magnesium content as well as having all the other nutritional properties of seaweed. Calcified seaweed controls the pH of the soil and neutralises it to pH6. This is a more reliable way to neutralise the soil than using lime, and provides a general fertiliser too. It has a low phosphate and potash content.

Seaweed meal

This is produced from bladder seaweed harvested from the coastline leaving the growing parts of the plant undamaged for further growth. Seaweed meal is expensive but is very high in nutritional value. It contains the major and trace elements as well as protein, carbohydrate, fat, the amino-acids, and many vitamins. It contains nitrogen and higher levels of potassium, but less calcium, magnesium and phosphate than calcified seaweed.

Seaweed liquid

This concentrated fertiliser is applied in a dilute form, either by spraying it onto the leaves as a foliar feed, to which it will respond quickly, or as a general fertiliser when watering.

Mineral Deficiencies

Mineral	Use	Symptoms of deficiency
Nitrogen (N)	Essential for the growth process of plants. Gives leaves a rich green colour – chlorophyll.	Stunted growth, yellow leaves. With older leaves – yellow at tip, yellowing down midrib.
Phosphorus (P)	Develops the root system, plant maturing and helps with the ripening of the seeds and fruit.	Stunted growth, poor root system – falls down in the wind and leaves become discoloured and falls prematurely.
Potassium (K)	Required for plant growth and development of fruit, e.g. tomatoes. Helps against plant disease.	Distance between the nodes is small. Yellowing of the leaf tips and leaves show scorching. Fruit pale in colour.
Magnesium (Mg)	Ripens seeds and essential for chlorophyll formation.	Stunted growth starting at the base. Leaves turn yellow and develop whitish stripes between the leaf veins which spreads upwards.
Calcium (Ca)	Promotes root and plant growth, neutralises the soil's organic acids.	Stunted growth, ragged tip to shoots. Roots do not develop and is susceptible to disease.
Zinc (Zn)	Formation of some growth hormones and in the reproduction process of some plants.	New leaves develop whitish areas each side of the midrib at the base
Manganese (Mn)	Functions in the plant enzyme system for plant metabolism.	Mottled effect on new leaves.
Sulphur (S)	Required for plant growth and maturity of fruit and seeds.	Young leaes are very bright green, veins pale. Fruits appear prematurely and remain small and immature.
Boron (B)	Required for water absorption and movement of sugars.	Root crops turn soft in their centres.
Iron (Fe)	Essential for chlorophyll formation and the synthesis of proteins in the cell.	Yellow tips to leaf shoots.

7.
PLANNING
THE
ALLOTMENT

The first move in directing nature's ways on your newly-acquired plot is to lay careful plans. These will help clarify the strands of information you already have, reveal some of the possibilities that you may not yet have properly thought out, and help you to form a strategy for the eventual productive use of the whole allotment.

You may like to produce three plans – the first showing the existing condition and layout of the land, the second a scheme of how the plot will finally be used, and the third a short-term plan taking into account the condition of the land and the time and money available to begin the work.

It is worth taking the time to make a reasonably accurate scale plan of the plot on squared or graph paper, by measurement and drawing. Once completed, this plan will be useful over the years when you have estimating quantities of plants to grow and the space they require.

The plan of the existing layout of the plot should have as much information on it as possible. First draw the boundaries of the plot – this is worth checking against the lease agreement to make sure you're not paying for more land than you've got. Then note the aspect of the land (the direction it is facing). This is especially important if it is on a hillside. You can find this out by either looking at a large scale map in the local library, using a compass, or asking other allotment holders. Check the direction of the prevailing winds. This is usually south-westerly, but they may vary locally. Wind is important to consider when deciding about the height of hedges, the need for wind breaks, and the planting of fruit bushes. Mark the height

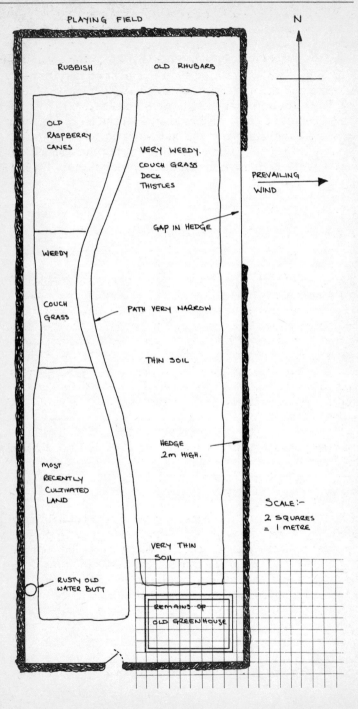

PLAYING FIELD

N

RUBBISH

OLD RHUBARB

OLD RASPBERRY CANES

VERY WEEDY.
COUCH GRASS
DOCK
THISTLES

PREVAILING WIND

GAP IN HEDGE

WEEDY

COUCH GRASS

PATH VERY NARROW

THIN SOIL

HEDGE 2m HIGH.

MOST RECENTLY CULTIVATED LAND

SCALE:-
2 SQUARES
= 1 METRE

VERY THIN SOIL

RUSTY OLD WATER BUTT

REMAINS OF OLD GREENHOUSE

and spread of the existing hedges, showing any gaps.

Show also the width and condition of paths, checking if they are riddled with pernicious weeds or smooth and wide enough for easy use of a wheelbarrow. Mark the position and condition of water butts, shed, greenhouse or cold frames, compost and manure containers, existing perennial plants, soft fruit, rhubarb, comfrey, flowers and lawn.

Soil conditions may also be shown on the plan, including thin soils, waterlogged areas, and variations in perennial weed infestation. To check for thin soil lift one spadeful of earth at intervals over the plot: the topsoil is thin if it is less than one spit deep.

THE LONG-TERM PLAN

There are two basic sorts of consideration in planning the eventual layout of the allotment garden – the practical and the personal.

The personal aspects include which crops you wish to grow, how much time and money is available, how much privacy you want from neighbours and passers by, and the balance between leisure and production. The gardens on our local allotment area vary from those in which every square metre of land is used for vegetable growing, to one with neat, high hedges enclosing lawns, grass paths, small beds containing a decorative mixture of flowers and vegetables, and a painted shed bedecked with honeysuckle and sporting net curtains!

The practical considerations include the existing conditions and layout of the plot, and the economical use of land and labour.

HEDGES AND PATHS

If the allotment has no hedges around it, the boundaries will probably be defined by paths. Wind breaks may be provided by growing soft fruit trained to a wire support fence parallel to the paths. Blackberries provide the best wind break because their leaves remain on the canes until the spring, whereas raspberries and loganberries lose theirs in the autumn.

If the plot is bounded by hedges then it is best to have paths next to the hedges for three reasons: firstly the root systems of hedge shrubs are extensive and take up large amounts of moisture and nutrients, so the soil near a mature hedge is likely to be dry and impoverished; secondly hedges cause deep shade, especially in winter and early spring when the land needs all the sunshine it can get to warm it; and thirdly, hedges need clipping, and paths provide access for this work.

The height at which the hedges are maintained depends on the need for security, privacy, shading, and the amount of work required to keep it trimmed. Thus the higher the hedge the more security, privacy and shelter it provides, but it also casts a greater shadow and presents a larger area for clipping.

GREENHOUSE

A greenhouse is useful but not essential for vegetable growing, and the new allotment holder may well have enough work and outlay to contend with for the first year or two without a greenhouse. However, most gardeners eventually need the benefits a greenhouse can provide, so it is worth including it in the long term plan.

The main consideration in siting a greenhouse is good light. It should face south; that is, the ridge of the roof should run east to west, presenting the largest area of glass to the sun. It should not be shaded by large trees, hedges or other buildings.

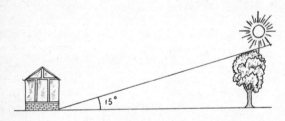

ELEVATION OF SUN IN WINTER.

Three other factors may influence the position of a greenhouse on your allotment:
- vandalism: greenhouses form an excellent target for the dedicated stone thrower as they are fragile and almost impossible to miss, so site it as far away as possible from any public land or right of way, or glaze the vulnerable side with unbreakable plastic.
- water supply: the most time-consuming job in the greenhouse is watering the growing crops, so allow space for a water butt next to it, and if possible site the greenhouse near to a water supply.

- existing foundations: on many allotments there are the remains of old greenhouses and sheds, and the existing foundations and brickwork may provide a good base on which to build. It is, however, just as well to consider their usefulness carefully. To build a greenhouse or shed to fit existing foundations may be more costly and time consuming than buying 'off the shelf', and the original siting of these buildings may not have been ideal.

GARDEN SHED

The potting shed is usually positioned close to or adjoining the greenhouse, but other considerations may influence its position.

The shed may be sited on a particularly poor part of the ground as long as the shade cast by it doesn't spoil an otherwise good area, or the top soil from the shed site may be used to improve an adjacent area where the soil is thin. Climbing plants can be grown over the shed to enhance its looks and provide a cut flower crop.

MANURE AND COMPOST BINS

Most gardeners have to rely on a yearly purchase of farmyard or stable manure to supplement their garden compost, and an area should be set aside for this to rot down and mature. The more accessible this is to the delivery truck the better, as it keeps initial handling of this heavy, bulky material to a minimum.

A moveable compost bin can be placed on any unused patch of ground, the juices from the decaying heap enriching the ground on which the compost stands.

THE CROPS

At last it is time to think about what crops you are going to grow. These can be divided first into two main groups – annuals and perennials – and later into much smaller sections. The annuals include all the vegetables which are incorporated into a rotation scheme and cropped within one year. The perennials include soft fruit, green manure crops, and the lawn, which all stay in one position for several years.

The perennial crops, once established, need considerably

less attention than the annuals, and the amount of land set aside for them may be influenced by the time you have available to devote to your garden.

The soft fruit bushes need plenty of space between plants and rows. Poorer areas of soil may be used once they have been cleared of perennial weeds, the land being improved only where the bushes are to be planted.

If you decide to have a lawn, it can go anywhere, although if you have an area of poor soil it could usefully be used for the lawn. A lawn provides a valuable green manure of clippings ideal for summer mulching, and a pleasant place to sit back and admire your own and nature's handiwork.

CROP ROTATIONS

A crop rotation is a traditional, practical planting scheme whereby the different types of vegetables are arranged in groups depending on their soil requirements, shared pests and diseases, and style of cultivation.

The vegetables are usually divided into three or four groups, and the land divided into the same number of equal plots. The groups of plants are then moved around the garden each year, thus avoiding a buildup of pests and diseases. The application of manure, fertilisers and green manures moves with the crops.

The number of groups depends on which vegetables and the quantity of each particular variety you want to grow. Your own plan will eventually have to combine your personal needs with the principles of good crop rotation.

The diagram shows a four-course rotation of vegetables, fertiliser and green manure. The four groups of plants are potatoes; legumes (peas and beans); brassicas (the cabbage family including broccoli, cauliflower, kale and swede); and finally root crops, including the onion tribe.

Rotation year one
Potatoes prefer a heavily manured acid soil (pH4.5–6.0), as this inhibits potato scab. Lime is applied after cropping the potatoes to neutralise the acidity of the soil. Potatoes are a good clearing crop for neglected land, as the bulky foliage and constant cultivation they require suppresses weeds. The land should be given a heavy dressing of manure or compost at least 5cm thick before the big, greedy potatoes are planted. The manure helps to retain moisture in the soil and is acidic. By the time the potatoes have been harvested, the

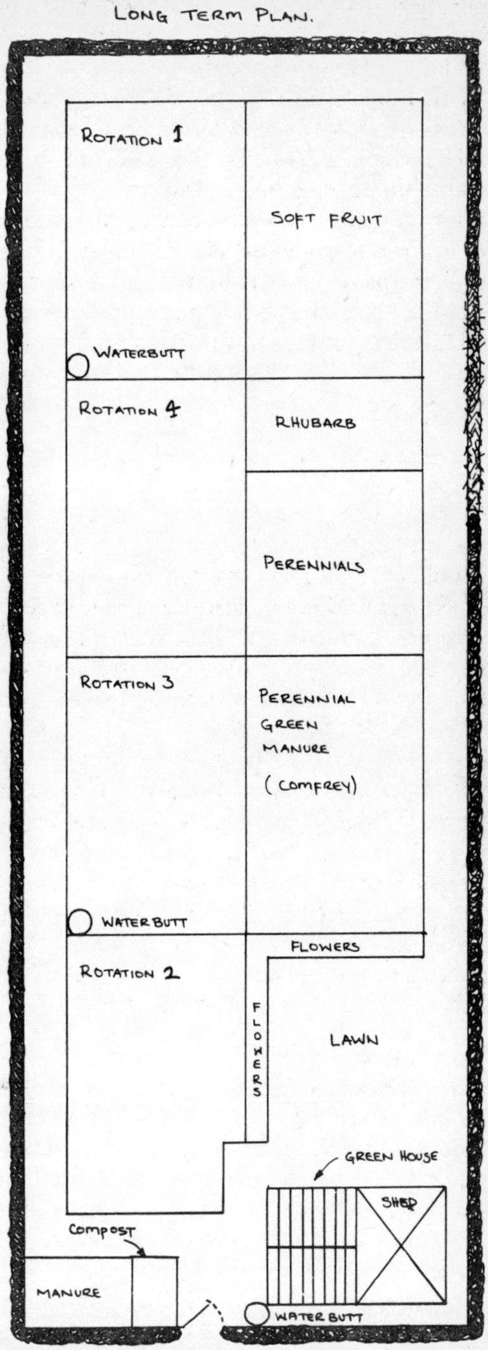

LONG TERM PLAN.

ROTATION 1

SOFT FRUIT

WATERBUTT

ROTATION 4

RHUBARB

PERENNIALS

ROTATION 3

PERENNIAL GREEN MANURE (COMFREY)

WATER BUTT

FLOWERS

ROTATION 2

FLOWERS

LAWN

GREEN HOUSE

SHED

COMPOST

MANURE

WATER BUTT

manure will be well broken down in the soil and there will be plenty of humus and nutrients left for the following crop of legumes.

Rotation year two
Legumes prefer a rich soil with a pH of 6–7. Bacteria which live on the roots of legumes fix nitrogen from the atmosphere, enriching the soil for the following crop. Lime, dolomite or calcified seaweed should be applied after the potatoes to neutralise the pH of the soil. When clearing the spent legume crops they should be cut off at ground level, leaving the nitrogen rich roots to feed the next crop. The legumes benefit from a mulching of garden compost or green manure which suppresses annual weeds, helps to retain moisture, and further feeds the growing plants.

Rotation year three
This is the year of the brassicas. The lime applied before the legumes helps to inhibit Club Root (a disease which can affect all brassicas), and it is most effective about a year after application. Also, the leafy brassicas enjoy the benefit of the nitrogen fixed by the legumes. The larger brassicas (brussels sprouts, broccoli, and cauliflowers) prefer firm soil, so these are grown where the peas and beans stood, without further digging. Use compost for the other varieties if they are not grown where the peas and beans stood, and dried blood or fish meal as a general tonic if the plants seem a bit slow.

Rotation year four
The year of the root crops. Large quantities of manure cause the roots to fork and become woody, so they are kept away from the heavily-manured potatoes. They thus come last in the crop rotation. Though called 'root crops', this stage of the rotation includes all the vegetables that don't fit into the other three years, such as spinach beet, marrows and courgettes, tomatoes and onions. The whole area may be given a dressing of seaweed meal and then the different crops treated individually.

The larger plants (courgettes, marrows, and tomatoes) may be planted in holes filled with compost; the spinach or spinach beet mulched with compost; onions, garlic and leeks fed with fish blood and bone meal and the root crops which dislike freshly manured ground simply left to grow on the humus from previous years.

ROTATION PLAN

VEGETABLES

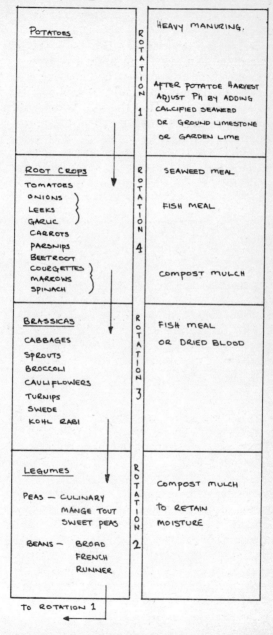

POTATOES	ROTATION 1	HEAVY MANURING. AFTER POTATOE HARVEST ADJUST Ph BY ADDING CALCIFIED SEAWEED OR GROUND LIMESTONE OR GARDEN LIME
ROOT CROPS TOMATOES ONIONS LEEKS GARLIC CARROTS PARSNIPS BEETROOT COURGETTES MARROWS SPINACH	ROTATION 4	SEAWEED MEAL FISH MEAL COMPOST MULCH
BRASSICAS CABBAGES SPROUTS BROCCOLI CAULIFLOWERS TURNIPS SWEDE KOHL RABI	ROTATION 3	FISH MEAL OR DRIED BLOOD
LEGUMES PEAS — CULINARY MANGE TOUT SWEET PEAS BEANS — BROAD FRENCH RUNNER	ROTATION 2	COMPOST MULCH TO RETAIN MOISTURE

TO ROTATION 1

VARIETIES AND QUANTITIES OF VEGETABLES

Your choice of vegetables and the quantities of each you need to grow are dependent on several factors.

There may be certain varieties which do not flourish in your area. Talking to other allotment holders can be very useful in discovering these local conditions, and the most suitable varieties to grow.

If the land is in a poor state it is not worth growing vegetables which need very rich soil, especially cauliflowers and hearting broccoli, until the fertility of the land is improved.

Crops which have a short harvesting period (lettuce, radish, summer spinach, summer cabbage, culinary peas) should be grown in very small quantities, or several small

Vegetable planting information

Rotation	Vegetable	Distance between plants	Distance between rows	Eating period	Good crop from 6 metre row
One	potatoes				
	early	30cm	45cm	July–Aug	15kg
	maincrop	37cm	50cm	Sept–March	20kg
Two	legumes				
	*broad beans	20cm	60cm	June–July	8kg
	*french beans	15cm	60cm	July–Oct	15kg
	runner beans	15cm	75cm	July–Oct	18kg
			double rows		
	*peas & mange tout	5cm	60–120cm	June–Sept	20kg
Three	brassicas				
	broccoli – sprouting	60cm	75cm	March–May	12kg
	brussels sprouts	60cm	75cm	Oct–March	10kg
	*cabbage	30–60cm	30–60cm	all year	10kg
	*cauliflower	60cm	60cm	Aug–Nov	15 heads
	kale	60cm	70cm	Nov–April	15kg
	*kohlrabi	20cm	30cm	July–Feb	10kg
	swedes	30cm	30cm	Aug–March	8kg
	*turnips	10cm	30cm	May–March	8kg
Four	roots				
	*carrots	45cm	30cm	June–March	7kg
	leeks	20cm	20cm	Sept–April	30 leeks
	marrow	120cm	120cm	July–Oct	20 marrows
	onions	10cm	30cm	Aug–March	10kg
	parsnips	20cm	37cm	Nov–March	15kg
	*spinach beet	30cm	45cm	March–Dec	15kg
	beetroot	15cm	30cm	June–March	15kg
Catch crops	*lettuce	30cm	30cm	all year	20
	*radish	–	5cm	April–Oct	lots
	*summer spinach	15cm	30cm	May–Sept	8kg

denotes successional sowing

sowings made every two weeks or so in succession. The vegetables which crop over a long period or are readily stored may be grown in larger quantities. A good selection of varieties will provide a succession of fresh vegetables throughout the year.

If your newly acquired plot is in very poor condition there may not be time to clear the weeds in the first year by digging. An example of a short term plan incorporating the methods of weed control given in chapter 11 is shown below.

FIRST YEAR PLAN.

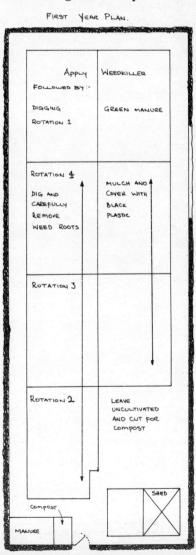

LAWN

The allotment lawn need not be a level, flat, perfect affair, just a place to sit or sunbathe, supply a little green manure and grow a few daffodils. It does however need to be weedfree, flat enough to mow without scraping off the top of humps, and free of stones big enough to stick uncomfortably into the tired gardeners bottom!

Remove the perennial weeds using any of the methods previously described. If you dig the land it must be left for at least a month and then trodden down before raking over to provide a fine seed bed. Ground that has been given the weedkiller or black plastic treatment should be cultivated with fork or rake to a depth of 5–8cm to create the seed bed effect. A dressing of bonemeal, one handful or about 60g per square metre would not go amiss. Compost or manure dug in, if you have any to spare, will only improve the results.

Choose a grass seed mixture to suit the situation, a rather slow growing mix with no perennial rye grass to limit the amount of mowing required may be best.

Sow the grass seeds at a rate of approximately 60g per square metre. It is important to sow the seed very evenly. This is best done by dividing the required quantity of seed into two equal portions, sprinkling one half working up and down the length of the site and the other half working across the width.

Once sown, the seed is covered by carefully raking it into the surface of the soil. Avoid watering unless there is a very prolonged dry spell, mid-August to mid-September being the best time to sow or April for a spring sowing.

Wait until the grass is at least 5cm high before its first cut with shears or sharp mower set high. As the grass establishes it may be cut closer to the ground and the clippings collected up for mulching or compost.

Occasional feeding with a general fertiliser may be necessary. Tea leaves provide a good lawn tonic, collected at home and sprinkled evenly over the lawn area to be taken down by worms.

If the hedges are overgrown or just higher than you want them then cut them back at least 30cm below their eventual height, then, as they regrow clip them enough to make them branch and form a thick mass of vegetation. Once the desired height is reached they may be maintained at that height by close clipping twice yearly, first in early summer and again in autumn.

PATHS

Paths need to be wide enough for easy handling of a wheelbarrow, reasonably smooth and firm. Some gardeners go to great lengths to lay concrete or flagstone paths. The benefit of this type of path is that once laid no maintenance is required. However, the time and money needed is great, and the result unattractive. The new allotment holder will probably feel that there is much more pressing work to do in bringing the land into cultivation.

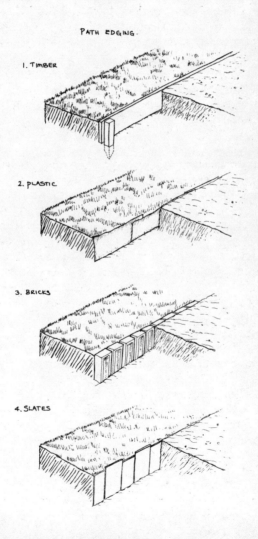

PATH EDGING.

1. TIMBER

2. PLASTIC

3. BRICKS

4. SLATES

There are two ways of establishing grass paths. The easiest way is to leave the ground uncultivated where you want paths, smoothing out the worst bumps and hollows and then either applying weedkiller and sowing grass seed or allowing the natural grasses and plants to establish, cutting with shears or mower when necessary.

The disadvantage of the second method is that many of the plants growing here will be weeds on the rest of the garden and will continually encroach on the borders of the growing beds. A barrier may be formed by setting in old bricks, slates or plastic, although these will provide a haven for slugs.

A better, though more labour intensive method would be to dig the land needed for paths, removing all perennial weed roots as you go, then prepare the land and sow grass seed as you would for a lawn, making the path 15cm wider than eventually needed, then cutting it back to the desired width after the grass is established and has consolidated the top soil.

The paths may be edged with old bricks, slates, polythene bags or timber to retain crumbling edges and deter weed roots from the growing beds.

In each case dig a trench deep enough to sink the edging material to the path level and about 1 metre long. Set the material in place and dig the next metre of trench using the excavated material to back fill the first section. Polythene and slates should be overlapped to stop weed roots, bricks should be laid upright or they'll collapse every time you dig near them. Timber is best treated with creosote to prolong its life.

Daffodil bulbs, planted where you will not tread on them will naturalise there, and provide a welcome early spring flower crop.

8. PREPARING THE LAND AND PROPAGATING SEED

Once the land has been dug it is best left for three or four weeks to settle before further preparation. If time is short then tread the ground before raking.

RAKING

The purpose of raking is to level the land and create a fine tilth in which to sow or plant. The soil is pulled and pushed around to the depth of the rake tines, working up and down and across the plot until the ground has been completely worked to this depth. Do not rake just in one direction or you will end up with a heap of soil at one end of the plot. You want to produce a fine even soil surface in which a seed furrow can be pulled without hitting any solid clods of earth just below the surface. Raking should not be rushed, but done with patience and care to provide the seedlings with a comfortable bed from which to rise.

RAISING PLANTS INDOORS FROM SEED

Some seeds may be sown in seed compost in seed trays or pots, in a greenhouse, in a cold frame or on a sunny windowsill. The seedlings are then pricked out into trays or pots using potting compost, then hardened off for planting in the open as soon as weather conditions permit.

There are two types of seed and potting composts. John Innes composts are soil-based. They are made from composted turf which is sterilised and mixed with sharp sand, peat and chemical nutrients. Soil-less composts are made from peat, and also contain a compound chemical fertiliser. The John Innes composts are generally cheaper than the soil-less types; however, the latter retain more moisture, encourage better root formation, and cause less root disturbance when the seedlings are planted out.

It is possible to make organic seed and potting compost by using worm compost. You will find a method for making worm compost described in a Soil Association booklet called *Worm Compost* by Jack Temple. This type of compost is too strong on its own to be used for raising seed, so mixtures should be made up as follows:

Seed compost
One part by volume sedge peat
Two parts garden compost (sieved to remove coarse material)
One part worm compost

Potting compost
One part sedge peat
One part garden compost (sieved)
One part worm compost
Half part perlite
225g of calcified seaweed per 9 litre bucket of mixture

Perlite is an inert mineral similar to vermiculite (the granules used for loft insulation), and is added to improve the moisture retaining qualities of the compost.

SOWING THE SEED

Fill a tray or pot with seed compost and gently tamp it down to within about 1cm of the rim of the container using a block of wood. Thinly sprinkle the small seed over the surface of the compost, barely covering it with additional compost which is gently firmed. Water the seeds in, using a watering can fitted with a fine rose. Cover the container with glass, polythene or cling film to prevent the compost drying out. Larger seeds may be sown singly in pots, or station-sown

2.5–3cm apart in large seed trays (to avoid the need for pricking out). They should be covered in the same way. As soon as the seeds begin to germinate, remove the plastic or glass covering and place the containers in as light a place as possible.

PRICKING OUT

If the seeds were broadcast-sown in their containers, they should be moved to new quarters as soon as the seed leaves have fully developed.

The seedlings should be transferred singly into 7cm pots or planted out in rows 2.5–4cm apart either way in boxes filled as for seed sowing but using potting compost. Take hold of each seedling by one of its seed leaves (not by the stem), and ease the plant out of the compost using a penknife or other implement; leave as much soil on the roots as possible. Plant them carefully but firmly in potting compost at about the same depth they were in the seed tray. When the box is full, very carefully water them in.

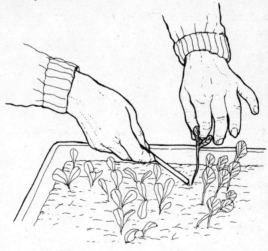

PLANTING OUT SEEDLINGS

POTTING ON

The half-hardy vegetables (tomatoes, marrows, courgettes, peppers and aubergines) cannot be planted out until there is no longer a risk of frost. They should be moved into 15cm pots when their roots have filled a smaller container, and hardened off for planting out in the first week of June.

About one-third fill the new pots with potting compost. Then, with a finger either side of the plant stem across the top of the pot, invert the plant and tap the rim of the pot on the edge of a bench or staging to dislodge it. Stand the plant in the prepared pot and work compost firmly around the root ball before watering in. At planting out time the plant can be removed from the pot in the same way, using the handle of a fork or spade which has been firmly pushed in the soil as an anvil.

DIRECT SOWING INTO THE SOIL

The depth at which seeds are sown is crucial; too deep and they will run out of steam before they reach the surface; too shallow and they will dry out or the birds will have them. The smaller the seed, the shallower it should be sown. If the soil is very dry, water it thoroughly the day before you plan to sow the seeds.

Start by marking the row with a tight line. Walking backwards and following the line use the corner of a draw hoe to pull out a 'V' shaped drill. The straighter the row, the easier it is to hoe between them later.

There are two methods of sowing the seed – either sprinkle the seed thinly along the drill, or sow three or four seeds at stations along the row with the recommended growing space between each group. The second method requires much less seed and less thinning out once the seedlings appear.

Once the seed is sown, use a rake to push the soil gently back into the drill. Then, with the rake held upright and its head across the row, walk beside the row and tamp the soil down gently.

Water the seeds using a watering can fitted with a fine rose. Finally, mark the position of the row with a stick at either end, and put in a lable, noting the crop, variety and planting date in your diary.

THINNING

Thin the seedlings to the required spacing as soon as they are through. The smaller they are the less the process will disturb the plants that are to remain. Some of the thinnings

CONTINUOUS   STATION SOWING
SOWING

SOWING SEED

FIRMING THE SOIL

may be used to fill gaps in the row; this can even be done with root crops as long as the seedlings are small enough and due care is taken not to damage the roots.

Do not leave the thinnings on the soil to attract pests (especially those of onions and carrots); remove them to the compost heap.

SEED BEDS

Some varieties of vegetables are better sown in a seedbed and later transplanted to their growing positions. This particularly applies to the cabbage tribe where the planting distances are so large and the number of plants so few that it is pointless sowing a continuous row. Lettuces may also be started this way and then a few transplanted at weekly intervals until they become too large to move. The 'check' (the disturbance they suffer when moved) will ensure a successional crop.

Prepare the bed where the plants are to grow as you would for seed sowing. Incorporate some peat into the top 7–10cm if you can. Sow the seed in rows about 20cm apart, thinning the seedlings to 7cm apart in the row as soon as they germinate. Make long enough rows so that you end up with a few more plants than you need after thinning, so only the best are used. Do not use the same spot for a seed bed each year but include it somewhere in the crop rotation.

TRANSPLANTING

Some root damage is inevitable when moving plants from one place to another. You can, however, take steps to reduce disturbance and checking to a minimum.

If possible, choose cool, damp weather to do this work, preferably in the evening. The soil in the seedbed and growing bed should be moist but not wet: in dry weather thoroughly water both areas a day before transplanting, allowing the plants to take up plenty of moisture and giving time for any excess water in the soil to drain away.

Lift the plants using a hand trowel, leaving as much soil on the roots as possible. Lay them carefully in a seed tray to transport them to the growing bed. Plant the seedlings firmly in their new position using a hand trowel or dibber, planting them deep enough so that when the soil is firmed around the roots there is a slight depression in the soil

around the base of the plant. Water the seedlings in as soon as they have been transplanted, giving each plant sufficient water to soak down to the bottom of the planting hole, and taking care not to wash any soil away from the roots. The depression formed in the soil around each plant will act as a small basin to stop the water running away from the plants.

In hot sunny weather some shading is beneficial to stop the plants wilting. This may be provided by covering them for two or three days with paper bags impaled on a stick or cane, upturned tomato boxes, flower pots, or large leaves. The larger leaves of brassica seedlings may be cut in half at transplanting time, thus reducing the amount of water lost by transpiration.

HARDENING OFF

It is essential that seedlings which have been started in a greenhouse or on a windowsill are slowly acclimatised to outdoor conditions. The easiest way of doing this is by moving them to a cold frame. Provide a little ventilation by propping the frame open in the daytime, gradually increasing the amount of ventilation until the frames are eventually left wide open all night. This should take about two weeks. If you do not have a cold frame, the pots and boxes of plants must be moved outside each day and brought indoors at night.

HOEING AND WEEDING

Regular hoeing along the rows and between the plants will defeat the annual weeds and maintain an open surface texture in the soil, where rain and sun would otherwise conspire to form a hard crust.

Hoe when the soil is fairly dry, and do not water for two or three days afterwards so that the weeds can dry out and die. The work is much easier when the weeds are still small, so hoe regularly. Don't wait for the weeds to form tough stems, strong roots and seeds.

Hand weeding will have to be done where weeds appear very close to the growing crops. Allow the weeds to grow a littler bigger than you would before hoeing so that they are easier to grasp and pull out.

Any perennial weed shoots which come up from roots which you have missed while digging need to be removed completely; hoeing the top off will not kill them, so dig them out with a hand fork. Perennial weed seedlings will generally succumb to regular hoeing as long as they are very young when the work is done (see Chapter 11).

The weeds may be left on the surface where they grew, collected up and used as a mulch or removed to the compost heap. Perennial weeds and any weeds that have been allowed to set seed should be composted.

WATERING

Watering should be done with as much care and consideration as any other gardening task. Although it is possible to over-water container grown plants, it is seldom a problem with those planted out in open ground. Under-watering is much more likely to occur. It takes at least 10cm of rainfall to thoroughly soak the soil. To supply an equivalent amount of water artificially means 10 litres or one large watering can full of water per square metre.

When watering-in seeds or newly transplanted seedlings, be sure to apply sufficient water to soak the soil below the seeds or roots. Established plants should be given enough water to reach the roots and keep the soil moist for several days. If too little water is given and only the surface of the soil moistened, the plants will be encouraged to form shallow root systems which will be damage as soon as the surface soil dries out.

HARVESTING AND STORAGE

Specific recommendations for harvesting and storage of crops are given under the individual vegetables. Some advice however applies to all vegetables:

- Only store vegetables which are in perfect condition – free from rot, bruises or insect damage.
- Take care not to bruise or otherwise damage crops when harvesting.
- Leave crops in the ground as long as possible, but avoid rot, frost-damage and over-maturity.
- If possible harvest in cool weather and keep crops cool.
- Store vegetables in a cool but frost-free place.

STORING ROOT CROPS

Harvest the roots and trim the leaves to within about 2cm of the root. Lay them in damp peat (to avoid dessication) in a box or tea chest, making sure that the roots are not touching each other. Cover each layer with peat and store the box in a cool, frost-free place. Newspaper may also be used to separate the roots.

9.
VEGETABLES

This chapter deals with the culture of individual vegetables. There are notes on soil preparation, sowing and planting, cultivation of the growing plants, pests and diseases, harvesting and storing. The intention of the information given is to show how to prepare the land and look after the growing plants to give them the best possible chance of providing a worthwhile crop. I have assumed that measures have already been taken to eliminate perennial weeds.

It is possible for crops to fail even if you follow these instructions to the letter. Weather conditions never suit all the crops you try to grow: a cold, wet spring can mean poor germination of root crops; a long, hot and dry summer could mean a wonderful crop of ripe tomatoes, sweet corn and courgettes, but lettuce and spinach may run to seed before you have time to eat them, and winter cabbage and sprouts may be stunted by lack of water.

As the growing season progresses, spend some time just looking at what you are growing. Watch how the weather, the soil in different parts of the plot and your preparatory efforts effect the different crops. Try to work out why one crop is growing beautifully while another fails. Keeping a weather diary throughout the season may provide clues to why a crop succeeds or fails. It is easier when working the land to prepare a whole area for a group of vegetables which require the same treatment than to treat each row individually. It is also important that the whole of each rotation area receives its basic preparation, since this has to provide for successive crops over the following three years. For this reason the vegetables described here have been arranged in their rotation groups. If you have favourite crops which you particularly enjoy growing, they may be given special preparation and treatment within a rotation for one season.

For further information about pesticides mentioned in this chapter refer to chapter 11.

CHOOSING SEED

The seed catalogues offer a bewildering variety of vegetables, each mouthwateringly described to make choice even more difficult. Prices vary greatly between varieties, the F_1 hybrids usually being the more expensive. F_1 hybrid seed is produced by the controlled cross-pollination of two varieties. The resultant variety is more vigorous than its parents, but its seed does not breed true, reverting to one or other of its parents. Controlled production has to be done each year and it is therefore not advisable to save your own seed from these hybrids.

Discover which varieties other gardeners grow successfully in your area and experiment with choices of your own. Over the years you will develop your own favourites for successful crops and flavour. You will also discover by trial and error whether you need to choose certain varieties which are immune to particular diseases.

ROTATION YEAR ONE - POTATOES

Many people would argue that it is not worth growing potatoes because they are cheap to buy. They are included in our rotation plan for several reasons to do with superior quality and usefulness in the overall plan. The varieties grown commercially are chosen for crop yield rather than flavour. Artificial fertilisers induce the tuber to take up water, further increasing the yield at the expense of flavour, and the growing crops are sprayed to prevent blight.

When planted on land that has previously been uncared for, potatoes act as a clearing crop. The cultivation they require while growing and the thorough digging at harvest time, combined with the mass of foliage which the plants produce, help clear and suppress weeds, leaving the land 'clean' for the following crop. Potatoes are tolerant of freshly-manured soil, although the manure should always be well rotted. They prefer heavily manured and slightly acidic ground – the acidity inhibits 'scab'.

Preparing the tubers
Buy your seed potatoes in January or February. Buy only certified seed from a reputable source to avoid importing disease on to your land. If you examine the tubers when they arrive you will notice that there are more 'eyes' – sprouting points – at one end than the other. This is known as the

'rose end'. Set the tubers out in egg trays or tomato boxes with the roses ends uppermost – this is known as chitting. If you get boxes from a greengrocer, choose ones whose corner blocks stand up above the sides of the box, so that you can stack the chitting trays on top of one another. Place the trays in a cool but frost-free place. Chitting the tubers enables them to start growing before planting, thus providing an earlier and heavier crop.

DIGGING METHOD

Preparing the ground
There are two basic methods of manuring the land for potatoes. The first is to spread manure or compost over the surface to a depth of about 5cm, then dig the land, incorporating the manure into the soil as you work. The second method is to dig out trenches a spade wide and deep where the plants are to grow, adding about 8cm of manure or compost to the bottom of the trench and covering this with 2.5cm topsoil before planting the tubers. The second method, although more laborious, makes more economical use of the manure, and will probably provide a better crop. The first method, however, ensures that all the land is manured for subsequent crops.

Planting
Planting distances:
- First earlies: 30cm apart in rows 45cm apart.
- Second earlies: 37cm apart in rows 50cm apart.
- Maincrop: 45cm apart in rows 75cm apart.

Planting time:
- Earlies: mid-March.
- Maincrop: mid-April.

Recommended varieties:
- First early: 'Sutton's', 'Pentland Javelin'.
- Second early: 'Maris Peer', 'Wilja'.
- Maincrop: 'Desirée', 'Maris Piper'.

Care should be taken to avoid damaging tender shoots. Before you plant them, the tubers should be debudded, leaving only two or three of the strongest shoots on the rose end.

If you have spread manure over the whole rotation and dug it in, then plant the tubers in holes 15cm deep made

with a dibber or trowel. On heavy clay soil use a trowel, as
the dibber will tend to compact the soil and the resultant
puddling may cause many of the tubers to rot. Plant the
tubers rose end up, and carefully cover with loose topsoil. If
the trenching method is used, push the tubers into the layer
of topsoil covering the manure and refill the trench
carefully, avoiding damage to the sprouts as far as possible.

Earthing up
When the plants are about 15cm high, draw soil up from
between the rows using a draw hoe, leaving the growing tips
of the plants showing. This process is known as earthing up.
It will protect the plants from late frost, smother annual
weeds, uncover perennial weed roots which can then be
removed, and supports the growing stems which will produce
stem roots to form more tubers in the ridge. Earth up again
about three weeks later, making the slope of the ridge as
shallow as possible so the tubers will not break the surface
and turn green. This second earthing up and the eventual
dense foliage will further suppress annual weeds, so further
weeding should be unnecessary.

Harvesting and storing
Begin to harvest the first earlies as soon as the plants are in
flower. Only dig as many as you need for one meal, because
the longer you leave them in the ground the larger the crop
will be. Always work with a fork along the side of the ridge
to avoid spearing the spuds, and remove even the tiniest
tubers. If these are left in, they will become very difficult
weeds in next year's pea rows. Once all the first earlies have
been eaten, start on the second earlies, again digging only
what you need for immediate use. If the haulms – the stalks
and foliage – have died down before all are harvested, dig
and store them as you would maincrops, but use them before
the maincrop store because they usually don't keep as well.
Wait until the haulms have completely died down before
harvesting the maincrop. Spread the tubers out on the
surface to dry for a day or so, but don't leave them so long
that they turn green. Carefully sort through the tubers and
remove any that have been speared or holed by insects or
slugs. Store the tubers in hessian sacks in a dark, cold, frost-
free place. After about six weeks turn the potatoes out of the
sacks and check them for rot. Remove any damaged ones and
refill the sacks.

NO-DIG METHODS

I have successfully employed two methods to grow potatoes
in a no-dig system. Both involve covering the beds with at
least 5cm of compost or manure. This work is best done in
the autumn to give the worms time to start their work
before the potatoes are planted. The muck spreading,
however, could be done at any time during the winter. Cover
the manured beds with black plastic sheeting held down
securely with bricks – this will prevent leaching and warm
the soil ready for planting. The first method of growing the
plants is to cut slits in the plastic at the appropriate
planting distances, and push the sprouted tubers through the
slits onto the manure layer beneath. The shoots will find
their way through the cut plastic. The second method is to
remove the plastic and set the tubers out in the manure
layer, which is then covered with a 30cm layer of straw. A
bale of straw should cover a bed about 6m x 1.20m. It is
advisable to buy the straw several months before it is needed
so that it can be left out for the rain to wash away any
herbicides which may be present. In no-dig methods the
tubers can be planted closer together than advised for
earthing up methods, because earthing up is not necessary
in no-dig systems, and a closer network of plants will better
support the mass of tall foliage.

A very early crop may be obtained by planting some first
earlies early in March under plastic, covering the row with a
polythene tunnel cloche to protect the foliage from frost.
Plant the tubers about 15cm apart because you will not be
waiting for the plants to mature; you will start harvesting as
soon as the plants begin to flower, probably in the latter part
of May.

At harvest time remove the foliage and draw back the
straw or plastic. The new tubers which have grown in the
manure layer can be picked up from the surface. It is as well
to lightly fork over the bed to retrieve the few potatoes
which will have grown beneath the manure. Any that are
missed are easy to remove when they sprout the next year,
since they will be very near the surface.

Some of the straw will have rotted down and can be left on
the bed to add to the surface mulch; the remainder should be
piled up and can be re-used on next year's potatoes, thus
reducing the number of bales which have to be bought in the
following year. If the potatoes have suffered blight it would

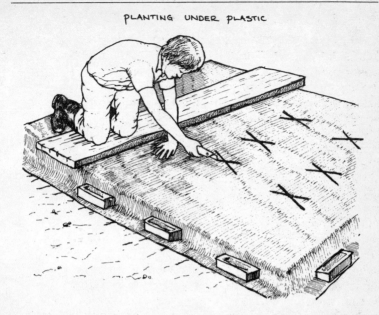

PLANTING UNDER PLASTIC

be better to compost the old straw and use it for a different crop.

The main problem with the straw or plastic methods is that they provide the perfect environment – warm, wet and juicy – for slugs. If they are a problem on your plot you may have to resort to slug pellets or fertozan slug bait (see page 139). Set out the bait or pellets on the manure when you plant the tubers.

There should be less need to water the plants using no-dig methods, because the straw or plastic mulch will drastically reduce surface evaporation. In a very dry season, however, water the plants through the holes in the plastic or through the straw.

Pests and diseases
Blight
This disease, which was partly responsible for the potato famine in Ireland in the 1840s, is most serious in wet summers. It first attacks the foliage, causing rounded dark green patches on the tips and edges of leaves, which become covered with a delicate whitish mould on the underside. The disease spreads throughout the foliage and the spores fall to the soil to infect the tubers, which develop sunken brown patches on the skin and quickly rot away completely.

Spray with Bordeaux mixture as soon as symptoms appear. If the weather turns dry and sunny this may stop the disease in its tracks. In damp conditions the disease can spread very quickly: either spray with Burgundy mixture and wait till the haulms die down before removing them to the compost heap, or cut and remove the haulms with shears. Some gardeners routinely spray the foliage to prevent blight, starting in late June in the south to mid-July in the north. Spray with Bordeaux mixture at three-weekly intervals.

Harvest and store the tubers from infected plants in the usual way but check the contents of the sacks at fortnightly intervals until you are sure that rot isn't spreading amongst the tubers.

Common Scab
Brown scabs appear on the potato skins, making them unsightly and difficult to clean. The disease is most likely to occur on alkaline soil deficient in humus; applying plenty of organic matter to the soil before the potatoes are planted and liming after the crop has been harvested should reduce scab to a minimum.

Blackleg
This bacterial disease may appear from June onwards. Some plants will appear stunted with yellowing, rolled-up leaves. They will eventually wilt and die; the base of the stems will be black and slimy. Dig up the plants and tubers and throw them in the dustbin. The disease is carried on the tubers, so buy only Ministry of Agriculture certified seed.

Wart Disease
This rare but serious disease causes a browny black spongy mass to form on the tubers, first around the eyes, later spreading to the whole potato. The spores can last 30 years in the soil, and the only remedy is to grow immune varieties – all good suppliers' catalogues will show which these are.

Potato Eelworm
This pest attacks the root system of the plant, stunting the haulms which yellow and die; the tubers remain very small. The eelworms are just visible as white dots on the tubers; they turn brown before dropping off into the soil. Each contains hundreds of larvae, which may rest for years in the soil before becoming active. Dig up affected plants and burn them or throw them in the dustbin; do not trust the compost

heap to kill them off. Growing a green manure crop of mustard may clear the ground of this pest; the root secretions seem to trigger the eelworms, which hatch but find no potatoes on which to feed. Meanwhile grow eelworm resistant varieties.

General hints
- Choose varieties which are resistant or immune to the pest you are having problems with.
- Allow the longest possible time before growing potatoes again on the same patch of land.
- Apply lime after the potato rotation.
- Use plenty of organic matter when preparing the beds.
- Buy only Ministry of Agriculture certified seed.
- Never plant locally grown tubers.

Although I have assumed that one whole rotation will be used to grow potatoes, other crops may be planted after the spuds have been harvested, depending on locality and weather conditions (for details of cultivation look under the appropriate groups):
- Strawberries can be planted after the early potatoes then cleared four years later when the potatoes return to this patch.
- Leeks can be grown in a waiting bed and transplanted to their final position after the early potatoes. Early peas or French beans could also follow the earlies to provide a late crop, although the French beans may have to be protected by cloches in autumn.
- Broad beans can be planted in November after maincrop potatoes, and except in mild districts protected by cloches through the winter.
- Green manure crops can also be grown after potatoes – mustard after first earlies, and winter tares or rye after maincrops are the most suitable.

ROTATION YEAR TWO – LEGUMES

Feeding the soil
Peas and beans form the basis for the second year of the rotation because they benefit from the manure or compost left unused by the potatoes. They prefer an alkaline soil which is detrimental to potatoes, so liming fits in well between these two crops, and the nitrogen-fixing root

nodules enrich the soil for the brassicas which are to follow. If the land was not manured in the previous season, some manure or compost will be needed to feed the pea and bean rows. Unfortunately lime added with manure will react with the nitrogen to form ammonia, so compost should be used. The new gardener is unlikely to have made enough compost to fill this need, so manure can be added in autumn and lime in spring. Alternatively, manure buried in trenches and calcified seaweed added to the surface at planting time should prove a satisfactory compromise. If you do have compost to spare, it may be dug in or used as a surface mulch once the plants are up and growing. Wilted comfrey leaves dug in or used as a mulch will provide much needed potash.

BROAD BEANS

Broad Beans are an easy crop to grow, being fairly tolerant of both soil and weather conditions. There are two main types – Longpod and Windsor; the former, which are hardier, are used for autumn sowing; the latter, which produce fewer beans but give better flavour, are spring sown.

Sowing the seed
Planting distance and depth: double rows 20cm apart; set seeds 20cm apart within the rows; 65–75cm between rows; plant 5cm deep.
Planting time:
• Longpods: October–November.
• Windsor: mid-February–mid-April.
Recommended varieties:
• November sowing: 'Aquadulce'.
• Longpod: 'Masterpiece', 'Bunyard's Exhibition'.
• Windsor: 'Unrivalled Green Windsor', 'Hylon'.

Soak the seeds for 24 hours before planting. Draw out two furrows about 20cm apart and 5cm deep using a draw hoe, and set the seeds out in staggered rows. Sow a few extra seeds at one end of the row to provide plants to fill any gaps left by seed which doesn't germinate. Mice love broad beans, but are deterred if the seeds are dipped in paraffin before sowing.

Successful autumn sowings can be made in the open in the south, but in colder area cloches should be used in which to overwinter the young plants. Sowings of Windsor varieties may be made in January under cloches, the cloches being removed in April when the plants reach the top.

Plant care
Most varieties are tall growing and may require protection against wind damage, especially in exposed places. Drive stakes into the middle of the rows at two metre intervals, and run string between the stakes and around the plants about 30cm above the soil. Hoe between the rows to keep down weeds, and mulch around the plants with compost or comfrey if you have any.

Pinch out the tops when the plants are in full bloom. This will discourage Blackfly who like the tender growing tops, and will encourage the flowers to set and the beans to swell. If the plants are severely attacked by blackfly, spray with liquid derris. Do this work in the evening to avoid killing the bees which will be busy on the flowers during the day.

Harvesting
The young pods, picked when the beans are only about 1cm across, can be cooked sliced or whole to provide a welcome early summer dish. Otherwise leave the beans until the pods are well filled before harvesting, starting at the bottom of the plants. When the crop is finished, cut off the stems at ground level and compost them, leaving the roots to enrich the soil for subsequent crops.

Pests and diseases
Apart from infestation by Blackfly, the only problem usually encountered by broad beans is Chocolate Spot Fungus, which attacks the plants if they are short of potash. Adding a potash-rich fertiliser such as wood ash at ½kg to 4 square metres before planting, or wilted comfrey dug in or used as a mulch, should prevent an attack. If you notice the fungus, water the plants with liquid seaweed or comfrey fertiliser to remedy the problem.

FRENCH BEANS

For those who really love French beans, a supply of pods can be available over a very long period by judicious successional sowing, and the season can be further extended by protecting the crops with cloches in both spring and autumn. The plants are tolerant of most soils, thriving in light soils and surviving where other crops fail in dry conditions.

Sowing the seed
Planting distance and depth: 15cm apart in rows 60cm apart, 5cm deep.
Under cloches: 25cm apart staggered in double rows 20cm apart, 5cm deep.
Planting time:
* Under cloches: early April.
* In the open: early May to mid-May.
Recommended varieties:
* Dwarf: 'Masterpiece', 'The Prince'.
* Climbing: 'Blue Lake White Seeded', 'Garafal Oro'.

French beans will not germinate well in cold wet soil, so wait until conditions are right, or warm the bed with black plastic or cloches before sowing the seed. For a successional crop, sow from early April under cloches and then at three week intervals until mid-July, with the first unprotected sowing early in May.

Plant care
Hoe and weed between the plants to keep them weed free. Mulch with comfrey or feed with comfrey or seaweed liquid fertiliser to provide potash. Earthing the plants up with 6–8cm of soil will avoid wind damage in exposed places.

Harvesting
Start picking the pods when they are quite small and cook them whole. Pick regularly, taking care to find all the pods which are ready. If any are left to ripen, the plant will stop flowering and put its energy into seed production. Keeping the plants picked, even if you have to give the crop away, will keep the plants flowering in an attempt to set seed.

Disease
Anthracnose
This fungus causes small dark spots surrounded by reddish hives on the leaves, stems and pods, which become sunken and later covered with a thin whitish crust. If the plants are affected spray with Bordeaux mixture before the flowers have set. Always rotate the crop. The fungus is carried on the seeds, so never save seed from infected plants.

RUNNER BEANS

Although these plants are fairly tolerant, they do prefer a
deeply worked, richly manured soil which will retain plenty
of moisture. Many gardeners take out a wide trench in the
winter and fill it with unrotted compost material, smashed
up sprout and broccoli stems and manure before covering it
with the excavated soil. The idea is to form an underground
compost heap to warm the soil and a layer of organic matter
to retain moisture. As the compost rots, the ground will
settle and provide a trough for watering later in the season.
In a no-dig system the growing plants should be given a
good mulch of comfrey, compost, grass clippings or sedge
peat to retain moisture.

Support fences
Traditionally, gardeners build a sturdy immovable
framework and grow their beans in the same place year
after year. This practice encourages the build up of
Anthracnose Fungus, and the fence should be collapsible so
that it can move each year with the rotation. Most gardeners
have to rely on bamboo canes as the framework for the fence
as bean poles are hard to come by. The supports can be
constructed in two ways as shown in the diagrams below,
using 2.4m canes in ridge 'tent' or 'teepee' form. Use thick
string for the intermediate supports tied to pegs driven into
the ground, which can be cut down and composted along
with the vines at the end of the season. The structure must
be very sturdy, as when it is covered by foliage it will be like
a sail to a summer wind. Stout pegs may be driven in at the
ends of the rows and guy ropes attached to the top corners of
the fence.

Sowing the seed
Planting distance and depth: double rows 15cm apart within
the row; 30cm between each pair of rows, using 'tent' shaped
supports 1.2m between each double row; 5cm deep.
Planting time: early May to mid-June.
Recommended varieties: 'Scarlet Emperor'; 'Enorma'.

Soak the seed overnight and sow the seeds on the inside of
the support fence, with one bean to each string or cane. Sow
a few extras to fill up the gaps in the row later. The beans
will not germinate in cold, wet conditions, and the young
plants are very susceptible to frost damage. Seeds may be

sown in early April in 7.5cm pots in a greenhouse or cold frame. Plant the seedlings out at the beginning of May, but protect them by fitting clear polythene around the bottom 60–90cm of the support fence. Half the row may be done in this way and the other half sown in the open, to provide a successional crop.

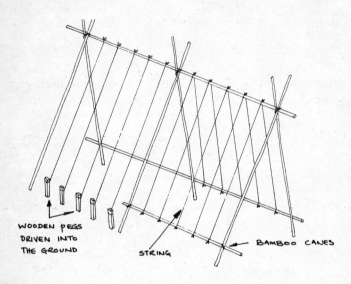

WOODEN PEGS DRIVEN INTO THE GROUND

STRING

BAMBOO CANES

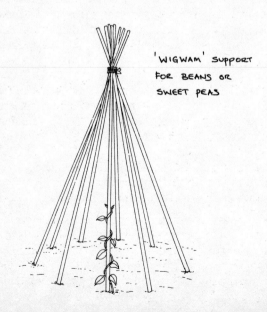

'WIGWAM' SUPPORT FOR BEANS OR SWEET PEAS

Plant care

The young plants may need some help to find their growing string or cane, but once they have begun to climb they will very quickly reach the top of the fence. Pinching the tops out at this stage will encourage side shoots to form. Spray the plants with water in dry weather to encourage the flowers to set (pollinate successfully and begin to form seeds). Water regularly, and hoe and weed to keep the row clean.

Harvesting

Pick the pods regularly before the beans begin to swell. Harvesting the crop young will encourage the production of more beans further up the plant, and will avoid stringiness.

Diseases

Runner beans share the same diseases as French beans.

PEAS

There is an enormous number of varieties of garden peas. They can be divided into three main groups: First early, Second early, and Maincrop. Mangetout varieties are grown to be eaten pod and all, and need the same treatment as garden peas. They all share the same taste as beans for rich, moisture-retentive soil, so if you have time to spare, and manure or compost in abundance, dig out trenches to incorporate a thick layer of organic matter to feed the plants, or mulch the rows once the peas are growing well.

Sowing the seed

Planting distance and depth: double rows 10cm apart; set seeds 5cm apart within the row; 60–90cm between each pair of rows depending on height of variety; plant 2.5cm deep.
Planting time: February–May.
Recommended varieties:
- First earlies: 'Meteor', 'Kelvedon Wonder'.
- Second earlies: 'Little Marvel'.
- Maincrop: 'Hurst Greenshaft', 'Onward'.

Soak the seeds overnight in water and dip them in paraffin before sowing to deter mice. The seeds will not germinate well in cold, wet ground, so wait until the ground is easily workable or cover the ground with black polythene two or three weeks before you intend to sow the seed. Early sowings will benefit from cloches, which will protect them not only from cold, wet weather but also from birds hungry for fresh new shoots.

Plant care

The seedlings may need protection from birds, especially wood pigeons who love the young plants as much as we love the peas. Black cotton string on twigs, or chicken wire bent into cloche shapes and placed over the rows, may be effective against really determined birds.

Provide the peas with early support: the sooner they have something to cling onto, the quicker they seem to get away. Start with small twigs followed by twiggy branches big enough to support the plants to whatever height they are expected to grow. If you cannot get hold of twigs and branches, build a framework with canes or poles and fix plastic pea netting or chicken wire if you can afford it. The framework needs to be strong enough to support the mass of foliage in high wind.

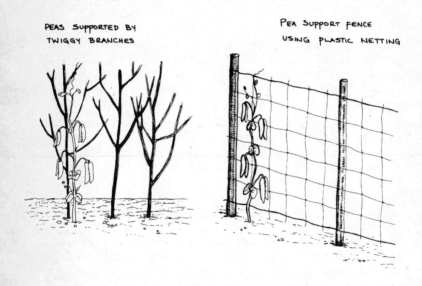

PEAS SUPPORTED BY TWIGGY BRANCHES

PEA SUPPORT FENCE USING PLASTIC NETTING

Hoe and weed to keep down weeds. Mulch the plants if you can, and water them in dry weather. When the crop has finished, cut the plants off at ground level and compost the tops, leaving the roots in to feed the soil.

Harvesting

Pick the first pods when the peas are still quite small. Open the pods and eat the peas there and then – they will be the best you've ever tasted. Pick regularly to keep the plants cropping. Mangetout should be picked while the pods are still flat, before the peas have developed – these too can be eaten raw and go well in salads if they ever get as far as the table.

Pests and diseases

Pea and Bean Weevil

These beetles eat semicircular holes out of the edges of the leaves. You are more likely to see the damage than the beetle because they operate at night. Dust thoroughly with derris or water with nicotine solution.

Thrips

These tiny insects attack the tender shoots, flowers and pods, disfiguring them and leaving silvery patches. The thrips will only be seen if the plants are shaken over a white cloth. Spray with nicotine.

Early varieties of peas and beans will be cleared in time to plant a second crop. Other crops that go well in this year of the rotation are spinach beet to provide leaves the following spring, turnips or kohlrabi for the late autumn, and spring cabbages. Some gardeners manage to fit in a catch crop of lettuce or summer spinach between the rows of early peas and beans (see under catch crops at the end of this chapter).

Green manure crops may also be sown when the peas and beans are finished – mustard after the early crops, winter tares or grazing rye to keep the land covered over winter.

ROTATION YEAR THREE – BRASSICAS

All members of the cabbage family, which includes Brussels sprouts, cauliflower, broccoli, kohlrabi, kale, swedes and turnips share one problem – Club Root. This is caused by a fungus whose spores can survive in the soil for up to nine years. The fungus attacks the roots and starves the plants, which eventually die or remain very stunted. There is no safe cure for the disease, but the addition of lime, a strict rotation for the cabbage tribe, and thorough weeding, all help to eliminate the disease. Even if the allotment has been uncultivated for many years Club Root may still be present,

CABBAGE CLUB ROOT

surviving on the roots of weeds such as Fat Hen (*Capsella bursa-pastoris*) which belongs to the cabbage family. Sprouting broccoli, kale, kohlrabi, turnip and swedes do have partial resistance to the disease. If the problem is very serious, however, you could grow only the more resilient varieties on half the rotation each year, taking eight years to use each patch in the hope that the disease will diminish. Any affected plants should be dug out to remove as much root as possible, and the plants burnt, as even the hottest compost heap will not destroy the spores.

The land should have plenty of organic matter and nutrients left from previous treatment, and the liming done before the peas and beans should leave the soil ready for the new crops. Broccoli and Brussels sprouts prefer very firm ground, and are best planted where the peas and beans were hoed off. If you must dig, then tread the ground thoroughly before planting. A top dressing of fish meal could be applied at about 100g per square metre as a general fertiliser.

SPROUTING BROCCOLI

These large plants produce small flower heads from the leaf axils in early spring, when other green vegetables are scarce. There are early and late maturing varieties which are sown at the same time and which, when grown together, will provide a harvest throughout March and April.

Sowing and planting
Planting distance: 60cm apart in rows; 75cm between the rows.

Sowing time: mid-April.
Recommended varieties: 'Early Purple Sprouting', 'Late
Purple Sprouting'.

Sow the seeds shallowly in a prepared seed bed in rows 23cm
apart, leaving enough room for hoeing between the rows.
Thin the seedlings to 7cm apart and transplant to their final
positions before they become too big and lanky. If possible,
do this work in cool weather to reduce wilting. Choose
ground where peas and beans grew the previous season and
which has not been dug. Plant very firmly and thoroughly.
Water the plants in.

Plant care
Later in the season, earth the plants up with 7–10cm of soil
to help them support their top-heavy foliage through the
winter. In very exposed places the plants may need staking
and tying to protect them. Hoe or mulch to keep the land
clean.

Harvesting
Start picking the side shoots when a tight cluster of flower
buds has formed. Break the stems off, leaving about one
third of the stem from which new shoots will appear. When
all the shoots have been harvested, the leaves can be used as
spring greens.

Pests and diseases
See end of brassica section.

BRUSSELS SPROUTS

The soil must be very firm for this crop or the sprouts will
not form tight 'buttons'. Plant after the peas or beans
without digging. Manure or compost is essential, and if the
previous crop had none it should be dug in in the autumn
and the ground left to consolidate over winter.

Sowing and planting
Planting distance: 60cm apart within the row; 75cm apart
between the rows.
Sowing time: March.
Recommended varieties: 'Peer Gynt', 'Citadel'.

Different varieties may be grown to give a successional crop.
Sow seeds in a seed bed and transplant the seedlings when

they are 7–10cm tall. Plant firmly with a dibber, and water the plants in. Shade the plants or cut their leaves in half with scissors or a sharp knife, if planting is done in hot weather.

Harvesting
Sprouts may be available from October to March. Start picking the sprouts from the bottom of the plants when the bottom leaves start to yellow, taking a few sprouts from each plant. At the end of their season the top of the plants can be harvested as spring greens. The spent stems need to be smashed up before putting them in the runner bean trench or onto the compost heap.

CABBAGES

Cabbages fall into three main groups – spring, summer and winter. They should all grow on any reasonable soil, but prefer land that has been manured for a previous crop. A poor soil may also be improved with the addition of a handful of fish meal per square metre raked into the surface before planting.

SPRING CABBAGE

Sowing and planting
Planting distance: 30cm apart in the row; 45cm apart between the rows.
Sowing time: mid- to late July.
Planting time: end September.
Recommended variety: 'Myatts Early Offenham'.
Sow the seed in the seed bed. Transplant when the space becomes available after peas and beans are cleared, so the crop acts as a link between rotations two and three.

Plant care
Apply 60g of dried blood per square metre to the rows in early spring to help the plants into growth after the winter.

Harvesting
Cut the cabbages before they heart, and use as spring greens. Leave only a few to heart up because they will not wait long before running to seed.

SUMMER AND AUTUMN CABBAGES

Sowing and planting
For a June crop, sow in a cold frame in February; plant out in March or April. Otherwise sow in seed bed in March and transplant in May.

Planting distance:
- Earlies: 30cm apart within the row; 45cm apart between the rows.
- Maincrop: 45cm apart within the row; 60cm apart between the rows.

Recommended varieties:
- Summer: 'Hispi', 'Minicole'.
- Autumn: 'Celtic'.

Plant care
Grow only a few plants from successional sowings as otherwise they tend to finish together and few will be needed in this plentiful season.

Harvesting
Cut the heads as soon as a good heart is formed; they will not stay in this condition for long before running to seed.

WINTER CABBAGE

These are probably the most useful cabbages to grow. They are hardy, and once mature, they will stand a very long time without running to seed.

Sowing and planting
Planting distance: 60cm apart within the row; 60cm apart between the rows.

Sowing time: March in cold districts; April–May in mild areas.

Recommended variety: 'Christmas Drumhead'.

Plant care
Hoe regularly and watch for caterpillars and aphids, which seem to prefer these cabbages to all the other brassicas.

Harvesting
The mature plants can usually be left in the open until you need them. In a very severe winter, however, the outer

leaves may rot, and it is advisable to dig the plants up and hang them upside down in a cold place where they will keep for quite a long time.

RED AND SAVOY CABBAGE

Sown in March and spaced as for summer cabbage, red cabbages were traditionally grown for pickling, but are equally good cooked, or shredded and included in a winter salad.

Savoy cabbages are the hardiest of all cabbages; some say that the flavour is improved by frost.

Sowing and planting
Planting distance: 60cm apart within the row; 60cm between the rows.
Sowing time: March, April and May for a successional crop.
Recommended varieties:
- Red cabbage: 'Red Drumhead'.
- Savoy cabbage: 'January King', 'Ormskirk'.

Plant care
Treat as other cabbages.

CAULIFLOWER

Unfortunately cauliflowers are not that easy to grow. They need rich, moist soil for quick and unhampered growth. Plant after a well-manured pea or bean bed with the addition of fish meal at two handfuls to the square metre raked in about a week before planting.

Sowing and planting
To provide a successional crop, seeds are sown at different times of the year. If you are sowing in a cold frame or under cloches, sow in September to plant out in March, or in January to plant out in April. Sow outdoors in early April and early May, to plant out in June and July.
Planting distance: 60cm apart within the row; 60cm between the rows.
Sowing time: March, April and May for a successional crop.
Recommended varieties:
- Red cabbage: 'Red Drumhead'.
- Savoy cabbage: 'January King', 'Ormskirk'.

Plant care
Treat as other cabbages.

KALE

Kale is a very hardy winter, leaf vegetable, ready for
harvesting in February and March when other vegetables
may be in short supply. It will grow on very poor soil and is
resistant to Club Root. The plants do better on soil which
has been manured for a previous crop.

Sowing and planting
Sow the seed in a seed bed in rows 20cm apart and thin the
seedlings to 7cm apart within the row; sow 2cm deep.
Sowing time: early April in the north to late April in the
south.
Planting distances: 60cm apart within the row; 70cm
between the rows.
Planting time: June to early July.
Recommended varieties: 'Pentland Brig', 'Hungry Gap',
'Asparagus Kale'. 'Hungry Gap' and 'Asparagus Kale' should
be station-sown at the spacings given above, as they dislike
being transplanted.

Plant care
Water the plants regularly during the first few weeks after
planting, and hoe or mulch to keep down the weeds.

Harvesting
Save this crop for the late winter by leaving it to grow until
January before the first picking. Harvest the growing point
of the plant at the end of January to encourage the growth
of side shoots.

SWEDE

This vegetable provides a good crop of roots to keep through
the winter, storing better than turnips.

Sowing the seed
Sowing distance: thinly or in stations 30cm apart within the
row; 45cm apart between the rows.
Sowing time: early May in cold districts; late May in warm
districts.
Recommended varieties: 'Marian', 'Purple Top Acme'.

Plant care
Thin the seedlings to 30cm apart. Watch for Flea Beetle,
especially when the plants are very young. Hoe regularly
and water in dry weather. Mulch with compost if possible.

Harvesting
The roots may be left in the ground until needed as they are
not usually damaged by frost. If slugs are a problem, lift and
store in peat (see page 75).

TURNIPS

Turnips are best grown quickly, cropped small and eaten
fresh, before they become coarse and woody.

Sowing the seed
- Spring crop: sow in March, in rows 20cm apart, thinning
  to 10cm between the plants.
- Summer crop: sow in April and May, in rows 30cm
  apart, thinning to 15cm between the plants.
- Winter crop: sow at the end of July, in rows 45cm apart,
  thinning to 30cm between the plants.
Recommended varieties:
- Early: 'Snowball'.
- Maincrop: 'Golden Ball'.

Plant care
As for swedes.

Harvesting
Use the roots whilst young and tender. Store winter ones in
peat boxes.

Pests and diseases
The curse of the cabbage tribe, Club Root, has been
mentioned at the beginning of this section because control is
attempted by rotation and liming, and there is no safe
fungicide to defeat it. Keep the beds weed-free and well
cultivated. Remove the stumps when the crops are
harvested, and clear dead leaves from the plants and soil to
the compost heap; otherwise they will provide shelter and
sustenance for many a pest.

Caterpillars
The larvae of the small white, large white and green-veined

white butterflies can all cause great damage especially to cabbage plants. Keep an eye out for the butterflies: if you see them you are sure to find the caterpillars a couple of weeks later. Either pick them off the plants or spray or dust with derris.

Cabbage Root Fly
This fly lays its eggs on the soil at the base of cabbages and cauliflowers. The larvae burrow into the soil and attack the roots; the plant wilts and dies. Ask other gardeners if the insect is a problem in your area. If you find out by losing your plants, fork the ground over lightly two or three times during the winter to let the birds get at the pupae, and the next spring take the following defensive measures against the pest.

Get some roofing felt and cut it into 10cm squares. Cut a 15mm hole in the centre and thread the root through this when planting. Green mineral felt is best used with the green gritty side down to dissuade slugs. The fly will lay its eggs on the felt and the grubs will perish.

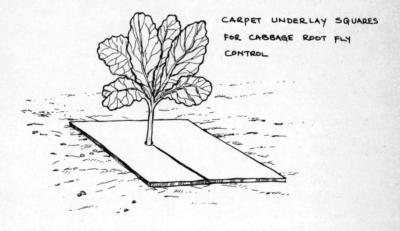

CARPET UNDERLAY SQUARES FOR CABBAGE ROOT FLY CONTROL

Aphids
A blue-mauve aphid colonises the undersides of leaves, particularly of Brussels sprouts. Dust or spray with derris.

White Fly
Usually seen as tiny white moths around the cabbages, the larvae look like small yellowy-brown scales on the leaves. Spray with nicotine and soap.

Flea Beetle
Flea Beetles usually attack seedlings just as they come
through and will easily destroy a whole row. Dust with
derris – it may be necessary to do this four times at three
day intervals.

CATCH CROPS

Most of the brassicas need a long growing season, but other
crops such as lettuce, spinach and radish may be grown in
the wide spaces between the rows of brassicas in the spring,
or follow after the spring cabbage or early turnips.

GREEN MANURES

Any spare ground may be used to grow green manure crops,
mustard in the summer and grazing rye over winter. I have
seen sprouts and sprouting broccoli undersown with clover in
the autumn (seeds are sown around an established crop to
grow on after the initial crop has been cleared), and hoed off
or dug in in the spring. Grazing rye could be used for
undersowing in the same way.

ROTATION YEAR FOUR – ROOT CROPS

This rotation includes not only the roots but also marrows,
courgettes, cucumbers and tomatoes, as only a few plants of
each are grown and they can be given individual treatment.

Root crops dislike freshly manured ground as it causes the
roots to fork and become woody, although it is safe to use
compost. The manure applied to the soil in the previous
season will be well rotted and will not cause this problem.
Apply calcified seaweed to balance the pH and as a general
fertiliser, or seaweed meal worked into the surface at 100g
per square metre before planting to supply potash.

Any green manures which have been grown over winter
should be dug in or hoed off well in advance of the root crop
sowings. Non-leguminous green manures should be sprinkled
with fish meal at 50g per square metre when they are dug-
in, to assist decomposition and avoid denitrification of the
soil.

BEETROOT

Prepare the land carefully to provide a fine seed bed for this crop, which may be grown to provide small tender roots in summer or large roots to store over winter. Fish meal added at 60g per square metre at sowing time will aid rapid growth.

Sowing the seed

Sowing distance and depth: in stations or thin to 15cm apart within rows; 30cm apart between the rows; plant 2.5cm deep. Sowing time:

- Summer use: mid-April.
- Winter storing: mid-May.
- For small roots in winter: July.

Recommended varieties:

- Early: 'Boltardy' (round).
- Maincrop: 'Detroit' (round), 'Cheltenham Green Top' (long).

The seeds, which are quite large, are actually pellets which contain several seeds. They are easy to sow in stations, two 'seeds' to each station, thinning later to one plant per station.

Plant care

Hoe or mulch to suppress weeds, taking care not to damage the swelling roots. If the seeds are sown continuously rather than in stations, thin first to 7cm apart and later to 15cm apart when the second thinnings are big enough to eat.

Harvesting

Pull the summer crop as you need them. The maincrop should be lifted by the end of October, the tops trimmed off (not too near the root), and the roots stored in peat boxes (see page 75), where they will keep for several months.

Pests and diseases

Beat Fly

This also attacks perpetual spinach. It lays its eggs on the underside of the leaves. The maggots hatch and tunnel through the leaves. A mild attack can be cured by removing the affected leaves and burning them or throwing them in the dustbin. A more severe attack will need nicotine spray.

Beet Rust
This disease also attacks all the beet family. Light and dark spots appear on the leaves. Remove affected leaves; do not leave discarded tops on the ground at harvest time, but remove everything to the compost bin.

Heart Rot
This is caused by alkaline soil and boron deficiency and should not occur on land which is properly fed with compost. However, borax crystals applied at 2g per square metre will remedy the deficiency.

LEAF BEET OR PERPETUAL SPINACH

This vegetable tastes very similar to spinach, is easy to grow, and a good supply of leaves is available for most of the year from two sowings.

Sowing the seed
Sowing distance and depth: sown in stations or thinned to 30cm apart within the row; 45cm between the row; plant 2.5cm deep.
Sow: April and August.

Plant care
The addition of fish meal at 60g per square metre before sowing, and a good mulch of compost or manure once the plants are established, will help produce a fine crop of large leaves on long fleshy stems. The autumn-sown crop (which stands the winter to provide leaves for picking in spring) appreciates a dressing of dried blood in March to help it recover from the long winter.

Harvesting
Pull a few leaves from each plant, taking only the outer leaves. Place your thumb on the upper side and at the base of the leaf stem, press downwards to break it off cleanly; this will avoid bleeding.

Pests
Beet Fly
See Beetroot.

CARROTS

Carrots fall into two groups: the small stump-rooted
varieties to sow early for a summer crop, and the large
tapered-rooted ones to grow as a maincrop for winter
storage.

Sowing the seed
Sowing distance and depth:
- Earlies: under cloches in early March; or outside in late
  March. Sow very thinly, 30cm apart between the rows;
  1cm deep.
- Maincrop: April, sow very thinly, 37cm apart between
  the rows.

Recommended varieties:
- Early: 'Early Nantes', 'Chantenay Red Cored'.
- Maincrop: 'Autumn King'.

Cover the land with black plastic or cloches two to three
weeks before sowing, to warm the ground. Do not make
outdoor sowings until the soil has warmed up: carrots won't
germinate in either cold or dry soil, so wait for conditions to
be just right.

Plant care
The main difficulty with growing carrots is to protect them
from Carrot Fly. This small shiny green insect is very
common, and attracted to the carrots by their smell. They
lay their eggs in the soil and the larvae burrow down to
infest the roots. First signs of an attack are noticed when the
centre leaves turn red and the plant wilts. Pull up the
affected plants and use any part of the root which is not
damaged. Throw the rest away. Insecticides are ineffective
because the grubs live far enough below ground to avoid
them; indeed, spraying will kill more of the predators than it
will the pest.

To limit the attack of Carrot Fly, thin the carrots in damp
weather firstly to 7cm apart, removing the thinnings to the
compost heap. Draw a little soil up to the remaining plants.
Make a second thinning to 15cm apart when the roots are
big enough to eat. Hoe or mulch to keep the rows free of
weeds but take care not to damage the roots when hoeing.

Station sowing or the use of pelleted seed to reduce the
need for thinning may further reduce the chance of

infestation. Pelleted seed must be kept moist in order to germinate. Sowing quick-maturing varieties in July for eating young during autumn will avoid the worst of the Fly which is most prevalent in June.

Carrot addicts could grow their crop under polythene tunnel cloches surrounded by a barrier, using woven polythene sheeting (available from garden centres) which will let in rain and fresh air but keep out Carrot Fly. Considerable care will have to be taken to ensure that the cloches or barrier are flyproof at ground level every time the polythene is removed for weeding or picking.

CARROT FLY BARRIER

If the crop has been attacked by Carrot Fly then fork over the land regularly during the winter to expose as many of the pupae as possible to the birds.

Harvesting
Pull the early varieties while they are young and tender; do not leave discarded tops on the soil to attract the flies. The maincrop is lifted before the first frost, the top trimmed off not too close to the root, and stored in peat boxes. Roots which have been attacked by Carrot Fly will not store.

Pests and diseases
Greenfly
These sometimes attack the young plants in early summer causing the leaves to turn yellow. Spray with nicotine and soap.

Carrot Fly
See under plant care above.

CELERY

This is not an easy crop to grow: the seeds need a temperature of about 18°C to germinate, and the plants require a rich, moisture-retentive soil in which to grow to without running to seed. Plants can be bought from garden centres or nurseries if you haven't the facilities to grow your own.

Sowing and planting
Sow the seed in a heated greenhouse in early March. When the seedlings are big enough to handle, prick them out 75cm apart into boxes. The plants should be carefully 'hardened off' before planting out.
Planting distances: 30cm between plants; 70cm between the rows.
Planting time: early June.

Plant care
Celery is usually grown in trenches because it must be 'earthed up' in order to blanch it. Take out trenches 45cm wide and 40cm deep, making ridges on either side of the trench with the excavated material. Fill the trench with a 15cm layer of compost or well-rotted manure, or a mixture of either of these and sedge peat. Cover this with about 10cm of good top soil. An application of fish meal at a rate of 100g per square metre can be lightly forked into the surface before planting carefully with a trowel. Thoroughly water the plants in and water them regularly throughout the summer.
   Earthing up is in three stages, the first in August when the plants are about 30cm high. Hold each plant to bring the stems together and draw soil from the ridges to about halfway up the plants. The second earthing is done about three weeks later and the last one in October when the soil

is brought up to the bottom leaves of the plants. The ridges should be steep and firm to avoid too much rain getting into the centre of the plants.

Harvesting
The celery should be sufficiently blanched about two months after the initial earthing up. Dig up the plants as required, taking care to replace the soil to ensure that adjacent plants are not exposed to daylight.

CELERY SELF-BLANCHING

This type of celery is easier to grow because it does not need earthing up. It is earlier than other celery, and without protection it should be harvested before the first frost. This crop requires a rich soil and the addition of a barrow-load of manure or compost per four square metres will not go amiss.

Sowing and planting
The plants need the same start as other celery.
Planting distances: 30cm apart within the row; 45cm between the rows.

Plant care
This type of celery is not so demanding as the trench grown varieties. Straw placed around the plants will whiten them a little and they should be watered regularly.

Harvesting
The crop should be ready by the end of August and last until the first frost.

CUCUMBERS

The kind of cucumbers we buy in the greengrocer will not grow outside in this country, but may be successfully cultivated in a cold frame or under cloches. Ridge cucumbers, which have smaller, rougher-skinned fruits will grow outside.

The ground can be prepared by digging out a large biscuit-tin-size hole about 25cm deep at each planting position. Half fill the hole with well-rotted compost or manure, and replace the soil to form a small mound into the centre of which the cucumbers are planted.

Sowing and planting

- Frame cucumbers: sow seeds in early April in 7.5cm pots at a temperature of 15°C, to plant out in early May.
- Ridge cucumbers: sow at the end of April as above for planting out end-May; or sow three seeds per station in the open in late May, covering each seed with an upturned 1kg jam jar, which is left in place until the plants are established. Thin to one plant per station.

Recommended varieties:

- Frame: 'Pepinex' F_1.
- Ridge: 'Burpless', 'Tasty Green' F_1.

Plant care

Cucumbers are surface-rooted, so mulch the plants with compost or sedge peat rather than hoeing them to keep down weeds, and maintain the moist conditions which they prefer. Water regularly, taking care not to expose the roots. Do not allow water to puddle around the stems as this may cause them to rot; the mound-shaped bed should assist good drainage.

Frame varieties

The growing point of frame cucumbers should be pinched out after six or seven leaves have formed. This is called stopping. Lateral growths should then appear from the leaf axils. Leave four of these to train to the corners of the frame, stopping each one a leaf beyond a forming fruit. A new lateral will appear, to be stopped again one leaf beyond the set fruit, and so on. Grow an F_1 variety which produces only female flowers, or pinch out all the male flowers as the fruits will become bitter if seed is allowed to form.

Ridge varieties

Stop the plants after six or seven leaves have formed, then pinch out the growing points as you pick fruits to encourage more to develop. There is no need to remove the male flowers of ridge varieties. Feed the plants with liquid fertiliser once a week to keep the plants in full production.

Harvesting

Cut the fruits before they are too big to encourage more to grow. Ridge cucumbers are much smaller and more prolific than the frame type, so crop them regularly.

Pests and diseases
Mildew
This may attack frame cucumbers in hot, humid conditions.
Spray with mildew mixture (see page 139), making sure you
wet both sides of the leaves. Increase the ventilation until
the mildew disappears.

GHERKINS

Gherkins are grown in the same way as ridge cucumbers.
The seeds must be sown *in situ* as the plants do not take
kindly to transplanting.

Sowing the seed
Sowing distance and depth: sow three seeds in stations 60cm
apart each way, thinning to one plant per station; plant
2.5cm deep.

Plant care
Treat as ridge cucumbers.

Harvesting
Pick the fruits when they are about 5cm long.

GARLIC

Although the garlic we buy is all imported, it is a hardy
plant, which, given rich treatment, will give a good supply of
cloves which will keep easily throughout the winter.
   Prepare the bed by adding 150g of calcified seaweed and
100g of fishmeal per square metre, lightly forked into the
surface in September, together with compost if you have it.

Sowing the seed
Buy bulbs from a local shop, and divide them up into cloves.
Choose only the largest for sowing. Sow the cloves in
October by pushing them into the soil. Cover them so that
inquisitive birds won't pull them up.
Sowing distance and depth: 15cm apart within the row, 30cm
apart between the rows; plant 2.5cm deep.

Plant care
The garlic will emerge in about three or four weeks, and will
stand even the coldest winter before growing again in early

spring. Hoe or mulch to keep down weeds. Apply a dressing of fish meal at 60g per square metre in April, and again in May.

Harvesting
Dig up the bulbs when the foliage has turned yellow. Lay them out on the ground for a couple of days to dry off, then tie into bunches and store in a cool, dry place.

LEEKS

Although leeks can be planted after early potatoes, broad beans or peas, they are included here because they are a member of the onion tribe and because those who like to grow large ones will need to plant them out before the other crops are cleared.

Leeks prefer a rich deep soil with plenty of moisture. They dislike acid soils so fork in 50g of calcified seaweed along with compost or sedge peat at a bucketful to the square metre.

Sowing and planting
For early crops, sow under glass in January or February, pricking out into boxes 2.5cm apart. Harden them off towards the end of March to plant out towards the end of April.

When sowing outdoors, prepare a fine, level seed bed with plenty of sedge peat forked into the top few centimetres, and sow the seed very shallowly at the end of March. Whiten the seed with lime so that you can see it on the soil, and aim to get the seeds about 2cm apart. The seedlings should be ready to plant out at the end of June.

Planting distance: 15cm apart within the row; 30cm between the rows.

Recommended varieties:
- Early: 'Lyon', 'Prizetaker'.
- Late: 'Musselburgh'.

The young plants are set out in dibber holes 15–20cm deep. The plants are merely dropped into the holes and carefully watered in, enough soil being washed down the holes to cover the roots. Some people trim the roots to about 5cm long and the leaves to 15cm long to make this process easier.

PLANTING LEEKS

Plant care

Hoe or mulch to keep down weeds. Fish meal applied at 60g per square metre about a month after planting and again a month later will be beneficial. Water regularly in dry weather, as drought often causes the plants to run to seed.

Harvesting

Leeks are very hardy and can be left in the ground through even the hardest winter, the only problem being digging them up when 'the earth stands hard as iron'. Start to harvest the plants from October, finishing in time to plant the new crop the following April.

Pests and diseases

Fungal diseases, rust, white rot and downy mildew are shared with onions and are dealt with under that crop.

Leek Moth

This little brown moth, about 10cm across, lays its eggs in April and May. The caterpillars bore tunnels in the leaves, which show as white lines. The plants will eventually die. Spray the plants with nicotine as soon as you see signs of attack. Fork over the bed after harvest to expose pupae to the birds.

MARROWS

Marrow plants grow in bush or trailing forms which are grown on compost mounds in the same way as cucumbers. Courgettes are a type of marrow and are included here.

Sowing and planting
Sowing times:
- Mid-April in 7.5cm pots in heated greenhouse and harden off to plant out in early June.
- Early May under jam jars.
- End-May in the open.

Planting distance and depth:
- Bush variety: 1.2m each way.
- Trailing varieties: 2m each way; plant 2.5cm deep; sow three seeds, thinning to one plant per station.

Recommended varieties: 'Early Gem' F_1, 'Green Bush', 'Zucchini'.

Plant care
Mulch the plants with sedge peat, compost or a thin layer of grass mowings at monthly intervals. Pinch out the growing points of trailing varieties when they reach 45cm long to encourage branching. Water regularly to encourage the fruits to swell, and to discourage mildew.

Harvesting
Pick courgettes when they are still small (less than 15cm long) to encourage new fruits to grow. Pick marrows regularly during the summer, leaving one or two per plant to grow on and ripen for winter storage. The ripened fruits will store for a long time in a cool dry place.

ONIONS

Onions are an excellent crop for the allotment garden. A large number can be grown to store and use throughout the winter.

The plants can be started in three ways – in the open, in a

heated greenhouse or from sets. Sowing in the open requires the preparation of a very fine, level seed bed. Planting sets – small bulblets prepared by and bought from seed merchants or nurseries – requires less perfect conditions and avoids onion fly because no thinning or transplanting is required.

Prepare previously-manured ground by adding calcified seaweed at 150g and fish meal at 100g per square metre worked into the surface. Rake the land to provide a fine, level bed.

Sowing the seed
If you have a heated greenhouse, sow in January or February and prick out the seedlings into boxes 4cm apart; harden off to plant out in April 15cm apart in rows 30cm apart.

Outdoor sowing
Sow very thinly 30cm apart between the rows, and thin to 10cm apart within the row. Sow from mid-February, as soon as the land is dry enough to create a very fine tilth. Sow very shallowly, raking the soil back by working along, not across, the rows. Firm the soil with the rake head.

Planting sets
Plant 15cm apart within the row; 30cm apart between the rows. Push the sets into the surface just enough to cover them; trim any brown stems which might show above the surface, or inquisitive birds will uproot them.
Recommended varieties:
- Seed: 'Bedfordshire Champion', 'Hygro'.
- Sets: 'Sturon', 'Stuttgarter Giant'.

Plant care
Hoe and weed thoroughly to keep the beds clean. Apply 50g of fish meal per square metre in June, and water regularly in dry weather.

Harvesting
When the leaves begin to turn yellow in August, bend the tops over and leave them for about 10 days before lifting the plants and laying them out to dry in the sun. I arrange them in old bread trays so that they can be put under cover easily in wet weather. When the foliage is thoroughly dried the onions can be plaited into 'strings' to hang up in a cool dry place to store until needed throughout the winter.

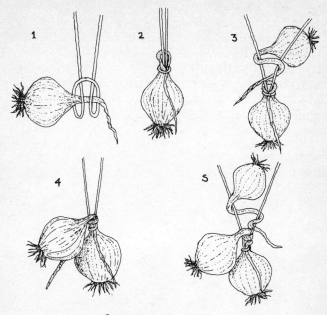

STRINGING ONIONS

SALAD OR SPRING ONIONS

These are sown in late August and September, on land that has been prepared as for maincrop onions. The seeds are sown thinly in rows 22cm apart and harvested by thinning the larger plants out for use first and so on until the crop is finished. Sowings may also be made in early spring, or sets planted out close together for a summer crop of salad onions. Recommended variety: 'White Lisbon'.

Pests and diseases
White Rot appears as white fungus on the base of the bulb; Rust as raised orange spots on the leaves; and Downy Mildew as grey mould on the leaves. For all these diseases, spray with downy mildew mixture or Bordeaux mixture. The spores can survive for eight years, making it difficult to avoid the disease by using a rotation.

Onion Fly
This small fly lays its eggs on the surface and the maggots burrow into the onion bulbs, ruining them. Dig up and throw

away infested plants. Dig the soil after the crop has been cleared to expose the pupae. The fly is attracted by the smell of the onions; this is particularly strong when thinning and transplanting is carried out. Planting sets which need no thinning therefore reduces the risk of attracting this pest.

PARSNIPS

This vegetable is quite easy to grow. If you have shallow soil then choose one of the smaller rooted varieties. Add calcified seaweed and fish meal at 100g per square metre before sowing.

Sowing the seed
Sowing distance and depth: 37cm between the rows, thinning to 20cm apart within the rows; plant 2.5cm deep.
Sowing time: mid-February–April.
Recommended varieties: 'White Gem', 'Tender and True', both of which are resistant to canker.

Sow the seed as soon as the ground is dry enough to work. The seed is slow to germinate so a few radish seeds may be sprinkled along the rows to mark them and these can be cropped when the parsnips are still small.

Plant care
There is little to do for this crop except hoe or mulch to keep down weeds.

Harvesting
Parsnips are very hardy and may be left in the ground until they are needed. Some gardeners say that the flavour of the roots is improved by frost, and wait for this before using the first plants.

Pests and diseases
Canker
This causes the roots to crack and brown rot to form. Grow a canker resistant variety.

Celery Leaf Miner
This tunnels into the leaves. Remove and discard damaged leaves. If there is a bad attack, spray with nicotine.

TOMATOES

Tomatoes are best grown under glass, but outdoor plants will provide some ripe fruit in most summers, and some varieties ripen well off the plants. Dwarf varieties may be grown under cloches.

Only outdoor cultivation is dealt with here as the greenhouse culture of tomatoes is a complete subject on its own.

Sowing and planting

In greenhouse, cold frame or under cloches: sow the seed in 7.5cm pots, three seeds per pot. Cover the pots with glass and brown paper.

Remove these as soon as the seedlings appear and thin to one plant per pot. Harden the plants off to plant out at the end of May.

Planting distance:

- Tall varieties: 37cm apart within the row; 75cm between the rows.
- Dwarf varieties: 37cm apart within the row; in double rows 37cm apart.
- Under cloches: 37cm between plants.

Recommended varieties: 'Ailsa Craig', 'Gardener's Delight'.

Harden the plants off very carefully, and delay planting if the weather is cold and wet. Prepare the ground as for marrows, with compost-filled mounds at planting distance. Take out a hole in the mound with a hand trowel and plant firmly so that the seed leaves end up just above soil level.

Plant care

Provide canes for the tall varieties at planting time, and tie the plants onto the canes regularly. Remove all side shoots which appear at the base of the leaves. When the plants have set four trusses of fruit, remove the growing top of the plants so that they can concentrate on maturing the fruit.

Dwarf varieties are neither tied nor disbudded but allowed to form bushes which spread on the ground. A mulch of straw will prevent slugs doing too much damage to the fruit.

Feed the plants regularly with comfrey or seaweed liquid manure.

Harvesting

Pick the fruit when it is well and truly ripe to get the best flavour. At the end of the summer, pick the remaining

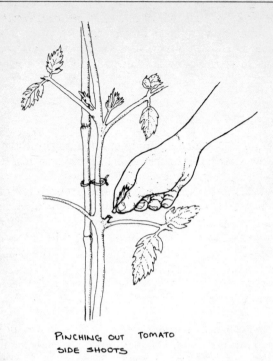

PINCHING OUT TOMATO
SIDE SHOOTS

unripe fruit and lay them out on newspaper in boxes in a warm place. Check them regularly to collect ripened fruit and remove any which have gone rotten.

Pests and diseases
Blight
This is the same disease that attacks potatoes. As a preventative measure, spray with Bordeaux mixture at fortnightly intervals from early August in warm districts, starting in September in cooler climes. Or, if you prefer not to spray unless absolutely necessary, keep a careful watch on the plants and, immediately there are signs of an attack, remove the affected leaves and commence the spraying regime.

CATCH CROPS

Catch crops are quick maturing crops, which can be grown between widely spaced rows of plants and harvested before the maincrop becomes too big. They are dealt with separately because they do not need to follow a strict rotation, since they are only on the land for a short period and do not share pests and diseases with any particular group of plants. They should, however, follow the crop rotation.

LETTUCE

It is possible to produce a supply of lettuces throughout much of the year by judicious selection of varieties, successional sowing, and the use of cloches.

Lettuces may be divided into several groups – summer and winter; cos and cabbage. There are also two cabbage types: the soft butterheads and the crisp iceburgs.

The summer and winter varieties need different soil conditions. Winter varieties prefer a light, well-drained soil in a sunny sheltered position, which has been manured for a previous crop with calcified seaweed at 150g per square metre and fish meal at 80g per square metre (added as a top dressing).

Summer varieties require a soil rich in organic matter in order to hold the moisture which restrains them from bolting. One bucketful of compost and one of sedge peat will suffice. This is used as a mulch, or is forked in together with the calcified seaweed and fish meal, as for winter crops.

Sowing and planting
Winter Lettuce
Sow in rows 30cm apart in late August–early September; thin the seedlings to 15cm apart and later to 30cm apart, using the second thinnings for salads.

Summer Lettuce
May be started in a greenhouse or frame as early as February, then hardened off to plant out in April. Outdoor sowings can commence in late March, the plants being thinned to 22.5cm apart in rows 30cm apart. The large cabbage types need 30cm between plants.
Recommended varieties:
● Winter: 'Winter Density', 'Imperial'.
● Summer: 'Little Gem', 'Webbs Wonderful', 'Windermere'.

Sow a few seeds at fortnightly intervals in short rows to provide a successional crop.

Using cloches to protect the autumn and early spring sowings will help to provide mature plants earlier in spring, when they are at their most expensive in the shops.

Plant care
Hoe and weed to keep the beds clean. Water in dry weather to prevent bolting. Do not cut the plants and leave the roots in; pull them and remove the roots to the compost heap.

Pests and diseases
Lettuce Root Aphid
This attacks the roots of the plant in summer. The plants wilt and die. Water with nicotine solution to save the still healthy plants and remove the wilted ones, which will not recover.

Botrytis
This attacks the leaf stems at the base of the plant, which turn red before rotting. The plant is later covered with a grey mould. Take care not to plant seedlings too deeply as this will encourage the disease. If the attack is very bad, sterilise the soil with formaldehyde, which breaks down quickly in the soil.

RADISH

Radishes will grow in almost any soil. Sow very thinly in short rows at fortnightly intervals from February to August, to supply plenty of small tender roots.
Recommended varieties: 'Cherry Belle', 'French Breakfast'.

SPINACH

This vegetable is not as easy to grow as the beet type spinach, but it matures quickly to form a useful catch crop.

The ground needs to be rich in organic matter, for spinach will quickly run to seed in dry soil. One bucketful of compost or manure with 100g of fishmeal to the square metre will prepare the bed.

Sowing the seed
Early sowings should be made in a sunny position from early March, 2.5cm deep in rows 30cm apart, with successional

sowings every three weeks or so. Later sowings should be made in moister, shady positions.

Winter spinach is sown at the same spacing, commencing in early August and then at fortnightly intervals till mid-September.

Recommended varieties:
- Summer: 'Longstanding'.
- Winter: 'Broadleaved Prickly'.

Plant care

Thin the seedlings to 15cm apart. Mulch with grass mowings, compost or sedge peat to maintain moist conditions. Water in dry weather.

Harvesting

Summer spinach should be picked hard and regularly, leaving only a few leaves on the plant. Only a few of the larger leaves should be taken at a time from winter spinach, to leave the plant with enough strength to stand the poorer weather conditions.

Diseases

Downy Mildew
Spray with downy mildew mixture.

CLOCHES

These can be used to grow catchcrops and considerably extend the maincrop growing season.

Crops that are to be grown with the aid of cloches can be divided into three groups:
- autumn sown seed; protected from autumn to spring.
- summer sown seed; protected during the autumn.
- spring planted seedlings; protected until summer or thoughout their growing season.

Cloches can also be used to prepare the land by warming and drying in a cold, wet spring, to protect crops from rainfall in very wet areas, to shield carrots from the dreaded Carrot Fly and to improve the germination of virtually any crop.

VEGETABLES

Vegetable crops grown under cloches

Vegetable	Variety	Sowing time		Planting time under cloche	Harvest	Period under cloche
		in open	under cloche			
French bean	Masterpiece	–	early April	–	June–July	April–May
French bean	Masterpiece	July	–	–	Oct–Nov	end Sept –Nov
Carrots	Amsterdam Forcing	–	January	–	late May	Jan–April
Peas	Meteor	–	early Nov	–	late May –June	Nov–April
Lettuce	–	August	–	–	Nov–Dec	end Sept –Dec
Lettuce	–	–	January	–	May	Jan–May
Courgette marrow	Zucchini	–	–	April	June–July	April–May
Tomatoes	Bush type	–	–	April–May	Aug–Oct	April–Oct
Broad beans	–	–	November	–	June	Nov–April

10.
SOFT FRUIT

Many gardeners will want to find room on their allotment to grow some soft fruit plants, which, although quite expensive and time-consuming to establish, need a minimum of annual maintenance and will provide many harvests of fruit to eat fresh, or to preserve for winter use.

This section deals with bush and cane fruit – blackberries, boysenberries, raspberries, loganberries, blackcurrants and gooseberries, and also strawberries and rhubarb. Few gardeners grow tree fruit on their allotments, and this large subject is not dealt with in this book. Those allotment gardeners who do wish to grow fruit trees should refer to Lawrence Hill's *Grow Your Own Fruit and Vegetables* for information on the growing of tree fruits organically.

Raspberries, currants and strawberries are all susceptible to virus diseases, and it is wise only to buy stock which is certified virus-free by the Ministry of Agriculture, rather than to accept offsets or cuttings from a neighbouring gardener.

It is very important that the land to be used for soft fruit is completely free of perennial weeds, especially those which have a creeping-root system such as couch grass or convolvulus. Once the bushes or canes are established, they should crop successfully for 10 years or more, and it is very difficult to clear persistent weeds from amongst the shallow roots of the plants. If necessary, work the land by growing vegetables on it for one or two seasons, until it is completely 'clean'.

Some sort of protection must be given to defend the soft fruit against birds. Bullfinches will strip currant bushes of their buds in early spring, and blackbirds and thrushes gorge themselves on raspberries and loganberries just before they are ripe enough for our taste.

Ready-made fruit cages, comprising a tubular steel framework and plastic netting, may be bought from garden centres or by mail order. Or a home-made cage can be

FRUIT CAGES

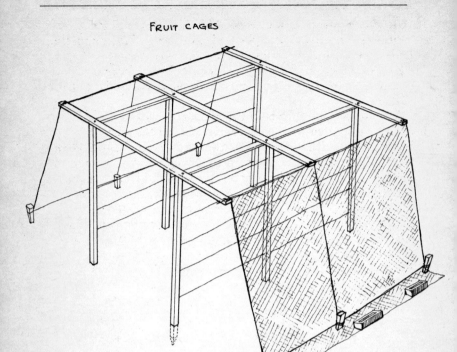

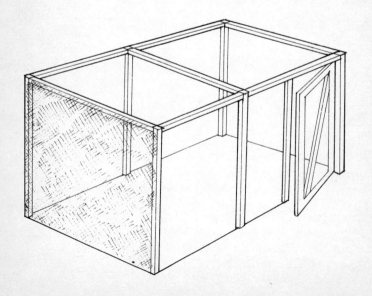

constructed, using new or second-hand timber and fence straining wire to support plastic bird netting. The traditional fruit cage is built as a rigid permanent structure, independent of the fruit support fences. I have built a successful cage using the support fences as the basis for the framework.

The timber posts for both the support fences and cage should be treated with preservative. Stand the posts in a bucket filled with creosote for at least 24 hours before using them. The pointed posts should be driven into the ground to at least 45cm and, once driven in, they should stand about two metres above the ground. Choose black square mesh plastic netting to cover the framework. This should be removed during the winter to avoid snow damage and allow birds access to insect-pests, and again when the bushes are in flower for bees to do their work.

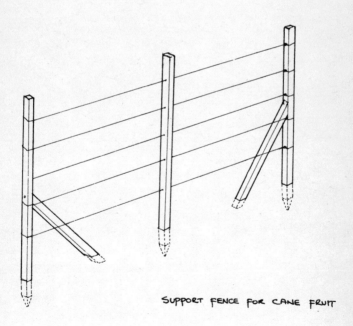

SUPPORT FENCE FOR CANE FRUIT

BLACKBERRIES

Blackberries will succeed on quite poor soil, and do not need heavy manuring. Prepare 60cm wide beds by digging to remove all perennial weed roots, and incorporate ½kg of a mixture of coarse bone meal and hoof and horn meal per metre. The rows should be two metres apart. Thornless varieties should be planted 2–2.4 metres apart in the rows; the strong growing variety 'Bedford Giant', which makes the best windbreak, should go 3–3.6 metres apart. Plant the bushes between November and March, shortening the stems to 40cm and tying them in a fan shape to the support fence. This severe pruning will mean that you get no fruit in the first year, allowing the plants to establish a good root system and strong new growth for the next season. The new growth should be tied in to cover the support fence.

Blackberries fruit on the stems which grew the previous summer, and also on older wood. Pruning should be done to remove any dead wood and keep the bushes tidy. In subsequent years, tie new shoots along the bottom of the support fence, then train them to replace the old or dead branches which are removed in the autumn. The prunings should be cleared away and burnt to destroy any pests they may be harbouring.

Recommended varieties: 'Oregon Cutleaf Thornless'; 'Bedford Giant'.

LOGANBERRIES AND BOYSENBERRIES

Loganberries are a cross between blackberries and raspberries, and boysenberries are a blackberry-loganberry hybrid. Both require the same soil preparation, initial pruning and training as blackberries. The plants fruit only on the one-year-old canes, which then die back and should be cut out at the base of the plant and burnt. The thornless varieties make this task much more pleasant.

Loganberries should be planted two metres apart and boysenberries three metres apart, with two metres between rows in both cases.

BLACKCURRANTS

Blackcurrants should be planted 1.2 metres apart in rows 1.2 metres apart, and on land prepared by digging in one barrow

load of manure and 1kg of hoof and horn meal per square
metre. The planting should be done between November and
March, setting the shallow rooted bushes out in wide holes
about 15cm deep, and spreading the roots out before covering
them firmly with topsoil. Prune the branches of the new
bushes just above an outward pointing third or fourth bud,
leaving the bushes to establish themselves without fruiting
the first year.

The bushes fruit on one- and two-year-old branches, they
need no pruning in their second year. In subsequent years,
after the leaves have fallen, remove about one third of the
oldest branches back to a strong young side shoot.

Mulch the plants with comfrey or garden compost every
other year, covering this with lawn mowings if you have
them.

Pests and diseases

Big Bud Mite is a microscopic insect which lays its eggs in
the young growth buds where they feed and breed, causing
the bud to swell up. They emerge the following spring and
are spread by wind and insects. The pest can be controlled
by spraying with derris-pyrethrum mixture when the flowers
are just about to open; but this practice will also kill any
creatures which feed on the mites. A better (though more
laborious) method of control is to examine the bushes closely
at pruning time and pick off and burn any oversized buds.

The Big Bud Mite carries a virus which causes a disease
in blackcurrants known as Reversion. This causes the leaves
to grow longer and narrower than normal, the flowers
become more brightly coloured, before fruiting badly, and
the plant to eventually die. Pruning out affected branches
will not cure the disease – the plant should be dug up and
burnt. A new bush can be planted in the same position, as
the virus is not transferred through the soil.

Recommended varieties: 'Wellington XXX'; 'Malling Jet';
'Seabrook's Black' (mite and virus resistant).

GOOSEBERRIES

Gooseberries require the same soil preparation and spacing
as blackcurrants, and a yearly mulch of comfrey and grass
cuttings or seaweed meal to supply potash.

When buying the young bushes, choose those which have

at least a 15cm stem, known as the 'leg', between the soil level and the branches, to allow access for weeding as the plants develop.

Plant the bushes in November in holes 7.5cm deep, spreading the roots out well and covering them firmly with topsoil. Prune the branches back to the third or fourth bud, whichever is pointing outwards, to prevent fruiting in the first year and promote the growth of roots and branches. In subsequent years shorten the branches by about one third to an outward facing bud, completely removing any small branches and those which are growing into the centre of the bush. The idea is to form an inverted cone-shaped bush which will allow air movement amongst the branches to discourage mildew, and give access for sunshine to ripen the fruits and enable easier picking.

Pests and diseases
The caterpillars of the Gooseberry Sawfly have a black head and a green and black spotted body with orange-yellow patches at either end. It is the most destructive pest to attack gooseberries. They emerge in three batches through the spring and summer, and can quickly strip all the leaves from the bushes.

Spray with quassia if you notice them early enough, or use derris, pyrethrum or nicotine mixed with soft soap, spraying carefully under the leaves where the caterpillars hide.

The Gooseberry Aphid attacks the growing tips of the bushes: the leaves curl up which renders spraying ineffective. Prune off the shoots and destroy them.

American Mildew is first noticed when a white mould, which later turns brown, appears on the branches, leaves and fruit. Remove any disfigured shoots, together with about 8cm of stem, and burn them. Spray the bush with downy mildew mixture.

Recommended varieties: 'Langley Gage'; 'Whitesmith' (mildew resistant).

RASPBERRIES

Prepare a 60cm wide bed by digging in manure and bonemeal in the same quantities as used for blackcurrants. In November firmly plant the young canes 8cm deep, 30cm apart, and in rows 1.2 metres apart. Shorten the canes to

PRUNING RASPBERRIES

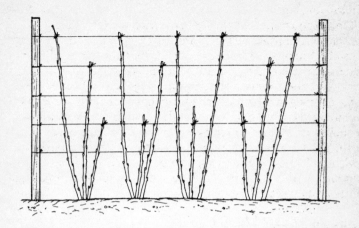

about 30cm and tie them into the bottom of the support
fence. The following spring, new shoots will appear from
below the ground. In the autumn the old canes should be
removed, and this year's growth tied into the support fence,
shortening the weaker canes to form a layered effect.

Weed the beds in the first year to keep them clean. In the
following years mulch with lawn mowings, comfrey or
manure in May or June, forking the mulch into the surface
in autumn.

Pests and diseases

The Raspberry Beetle larvae feed on the flowers before
burrowing into the young fruit. Spray with pyrethrum or
quassia, in the evening, 10 days after the first flowers have
opened, and again 10 days later.

The Raspberry Moth larvae tunnel into the canes, which
wilt and wither. Cut out the damaged canes and burn them.
The small moths, which are purple-brown in colour with
yellow spots on the fore-wings, fly in daytime and may be
caught on treacle-covered boards set out to trap them.

Raspberries may be affected by several diseases: Spur
Blight affects the buds of new canes; Cane Spot causes small
purple spots on leaves and canes in early summer; and Cane
Blight causes the canes to wilt in summer. Treat all these
three diseases by cutting out the affected canes well below
ground level and burning them, spraying the remaining

canes with Bordeaux mixture, repeating the spraying next spring as the buds open. Raspberry Mildew, which may also attack other fruit, should be sprayed with downy mildew mixture.

Recommended varieties: the large fruited Malling varieties may be grown to provide a succession of fruit:
- Early: 'Malling Promise'.
- Mid-season: 'Malling Jewel'.
- Late: 'Malling Admiral'.

RHUBARB

Rhubarb plants will crop well for about 15 years, so prepare the bed by digging in one kilogram of coarse bonemeal, one barrowload of manure or compost, and one barrowload of feathers or mattress stuffing to each square metre.

In winter, plant the crowns 70cm apart each way, with the bud just above the surface. Leave the plants to establish without picking any leaves during the first year. Clear any dead leaves in late autumn and mulch the bed with 250g of bonemeal per square metre and 30cm of dead leaves, covered in netting.

The rhubarb can be forced by covering it with a bottomless bucket in late winter or early spring, removing the bucket when the stems reach the top. Do not force rhubarb plants until their third year. Pick a few stems from each plant by pulling them off at the base, and stop picking after the beginning of July, to allow the plants to gain strength for the next season.

Recommended varieties: 'Hawkes Champagne'; 'Tumberly Early'.

STRAWBERRIES

Strawberries are best planted in August or September, giving them plenty of time to establish and crop the following summer. The plants only crop heavily for about four years, so they may be included in the vegetable crop rotation, planting them after the early potatoes each year and digging them in before the potatoes return to the bed four years later.

Prepare the bed by digging in a barrowload of manure or compost with 1kg of coarse bonemeal per three square

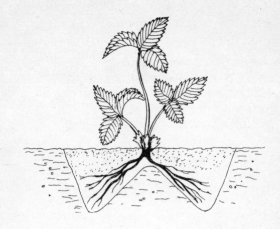

metres, and rake the bed to produce a fine tilth. The plants
are spaced 30cm apart in rows 60cm apart. Make holes for
the plants about 10cm wide and 5cm deep with a slight
mound in the middle, placing them on the mound and
spreading the roots out around it. Cover them very firmly
with soil leaving the 'crown' of the plant above ground.

Hoe to keep the weeds down, and mulch the bed in spring
with peat or straw to protect the fruit from slugs. Provide
netting to keep blackbirds and thrushes at bay – these birds
will spend hours trying to find a way through the nets so
take great care not to leave spaces at ground level. Once
inside the 'cage', and full of strawberries, the birds panic and
become entangled in the netting in their attempts to escape.

In the autumn remove the runners, using the best to start
a new bed. Clear away any dead leaves and burn them.

Pests and diseases
The Strawberry Aphid (which carries the Yellow-Edge and
Crinkle Viruses) is the worst problem to affect strawberries.
Drench the underside of the leaves and the crowns with a
nicotine and soap wash in April and May, or spray with
pyrethrum or quassia in the evening once the flowers are
open.

Grey Mould affects the foliage and fruit of strawberries.
Remove and destroy any damaged fruit and dust the plants
with flowers of sulphur.

Buying only certified disease-free stock combined with crop rotation, careful soil preparation and tidiness, should keep the strawberry patch trouble-free.

There are three types of strawberries: Maincrop which fruit in June and July; Perpetual, which fruit from June to October; and Alpines, which have small fruit, and fruit between June and the first frost.

Recommended varieties:

- Maincrop: 'Royal Sovereign' (early); 'Cambridge Rival' (early, mildew resistant); 'Cambridge Late Pine' (mid-season, virus resistant); 'Talisman' (late, resistant to root rot and mildew).
- Perpetual: 'La Sans Rivalle' (tolerant of light or chalky soils).
- Alpines: 'Alexandria' (propagated from seed).

11.
WEEDS, PESTS AND FRIENDS

For many gardeners, weeds are a constant nightmare. Many hours are spent trying to rid the garden of weeds which constantly reappear and grow at a tremendous rate. It is best to try and keep an allotment free of weeds, though weed seeds may lie dormant in the soil for several years and then germinate when the conditions are right. Seeds are blown onto the land or brought in with manure, and compete with the cultivated crops for nutrients and elements.

Weeds are host to pests and diseases during the winter which invade your vegetable crops in spring. Blackfly, for example, overwinters on fat hen and black nightshade, then migrates to beans, beetroot and spinach in the summer. It is therefore very important to keep the land as weed-free as possible throughout the year.

Weeds, like other plants, require particular growing conditions, and can be used as an indicator of soil conditions such as acidity and alkalinity, mineral content and deficiencies. If a great variety of weeds grow in your allotment, then the soil is likely to be relatively fertile.

In acid soils you will find some or all of the following: spurrey, corn camomile, henbit, sheeps sorrel, wild radish, black bindweed, small nettle, annual mercury, common storks bill, and shepherds cress. In alkaline soils you may find some or all of the following: common mouse-ear, chickweed, fumitory, corn poppy, wild carrot, hoary plantain, and night-flowering campion. In good balanced loamy soil you may find common forget-me-not, coltsfoot, field milk thistle, spiny milk thistle, stinking mayweed, curled dock, creeping thistle, goosegrass, yarrow, field penny-cress, sun spurge and long-headed poppy.

Other weeds are prevalent on derelict and uncultivated

land. The first to colonise derelict land are nettles (which are rich in calcium), thistles, cow parsley, hemlock, and rose-bay willow-herb. All these have deep rooting systems which bring minerals to the surface. These weeds can be put to good use if they are cut when fairly large but before they have flowered or seeded. Put them on the compost heap, where they will add plenty of bulk and nutrients.

Rushes on the land indicate poor drainage. Horsetails indicate that the subsoil is near the surface and that the land is poorly drained. Horsetails will disappear when humus is added to the soil, as this will improve the soil structure and drainage.

Docks indicate that the soil is rich in nutrients, and goosegrass indicates a good loam, rich in nutrients and humus. Black bindweed prefers nutrient-rich soil with a moderately acidic loam. Buttercups indicate that the soil is rich in minerals. They exude a substance which retards the growth and development of neighbouring plants.

Weeds can be divided into annuals and perennials. Annual weeds grow from seed; they flower, set seed and die in one year. They can easily be removed by pulling them up or by hoeing, which cuts the heads off the growing plants and kills the roots below. It is important to cut the weeds before they go to seed: 'One year's seed is seven years' weeds'. These annual weeds can be controlled by planting crops closer together so that the leaves shade the soil and prevent the weed seed in the soil from germinating.

Perennial weeds are more difficult to kill than annual weeds. The growing plant above ground can be cut off, but the roots beneath the soil store food and can send up new shoots. This can continue for years, and the only way to remove the perennial weed completely is to dig out the whole plant together with its root system, though it is a labourious task.

Weeds should be left to dry out for 48 hours before putting them on the compost heap so that they becoming a soggy moss.

Some perennial weeds can be controlled by cutting them regularly over one or two seasons. Ground elder, for instance, will die after two years if it is cut every 28 days, and bracken and nettles will die if they are cut three times in one season. The traditional method to clear couch grass is to rotovate the land then leave it till the couch starts to grow again; rotovate a second time and then a third. The couch roots should now be exhausted and the ground ready for planting.

Apart from digging, there are several methods of defeating perennial weeds. By far the quickest method is to apply weedkiller! Although this practice is frowned upon by most organic gardeners, and may be expensive, there are compounds on the market which break down quickly and harmlessly in the soil. It is worth checking the label before buying to make sure the one you choose is effective against the weeds on your plot. Ammonium sulphanate [Amcide] is probably the best. This breaks down into sulphate of ammonia in about four weeks, and is harmless to birds and insects. It is available from the Henry Doubleday Research Association.

Black plastic sheeting (available from DIY superstores), spread over the weedy ground and weighted down with old bricks for a year, has been effective on my garden, controlling everything except horsetail.

If you have an area of land that you want to leave untouched in the first year, cut the weeds down before they flower and compost them – this will keep your landlord and neighbours happy, the compost bin full, and prevent the spread of seeds to your cultivated land.

It is very difficult to estimate how long it will take to dig and clear the soil until you actually start. The speed of the work varies according to soil conditions and weed type, and the weather. If your digging schedule proves over-ambitious you can fall back on the less labour-intensive methods.

Some weeds are beneficial to the garden. A small patch of nettles in the corner will attract butterflies and other wildlife, which help to maintain the balance of your garden ecosystem. Since 1945 the introduction of a vast range of chemical fertilizers, herbicides, and pesticides has greatly increased crop production in the West. Today pesticides are poured onto the land globally at a rate of 2,500 million kg every year – ½kg for every human being. This carefree use of chemicals is not only very expensive; it also pollutes the food we eat and our water supply, and disrupts the balance of ecosystems which have developed over millions of years.

Although we have included details about organic pesticides, we believe they should only be used as a last resort. In general it is better to use other means to deter pests wherever possible, and even tolerate a few which provide food for the insect predators.

The combination of crop rotation, the addition of plenty of humus-making material to the soil, correct acid/alkali balance, and the encouragement of pest predators will reduce the problems of pests and diseases, as well as producing strong, healthy plants which are better able to withstand an attack. We very rarely use any pesticides, preferring to grow vegetables which will survive in our garden without the aid of chemicals. Large caterpillars and grubs can be picked off the plants by hand and destroyed, leaves affected by tunnelling insects such as leaf miner can be removed and destroyed. Any plants which are incurably infested or diseased should be dug up and burnt, or removed from the site. Resistant varieties should be grown in the future. Protection can be given by providing a physical barrier around plants – use plastic netting, or webs of black cotton or chicken wire to protect young brassica plants and pea seedlings from birds, and you can protect seedlings from slugs and cutworms by cutting 5cm collars from plastic lemonade containers and pushing them half into the soil around the seedlings. We cannot grow carrots on our allotment unless they are enclosed by mini tunnel cloches covered with 0.75mm polythene netting (Papronet) or surrounded by a 75cm high Papronet barrier.

The soil is inhabited by a myriad of living things, some beneficial and some harmful to plants. It is often difficult to distinguish between them. A general rule is that fast moving creatures are beneficial and slow-moving ones are harmful – apart from worms.

SOME GARDENER'S FRIENDS

Although some crops need protection from birds, birds are otherwise very useful friends, consuming many insect pests which would otherwise damage crops.

Hedgehogs eat a great variety of insects, slugs, cutworms, woodlice and millipedes. If you are lucky enough to have one on your plot, encourage it to stay.

Ladybirds and their slate grey, spotted larvae (which may be mistaken for pests) eat vast quantities of aphids.

Bees and wasps are both pollinatores, and are encouraged into the garden by flowers. Wasps eat greenfly and other small flies. Hoverflies are similar to small wasps. They are about 1cm long, have a black and yellow striped thorax, and can hover in one place. They are important pollinators. Their

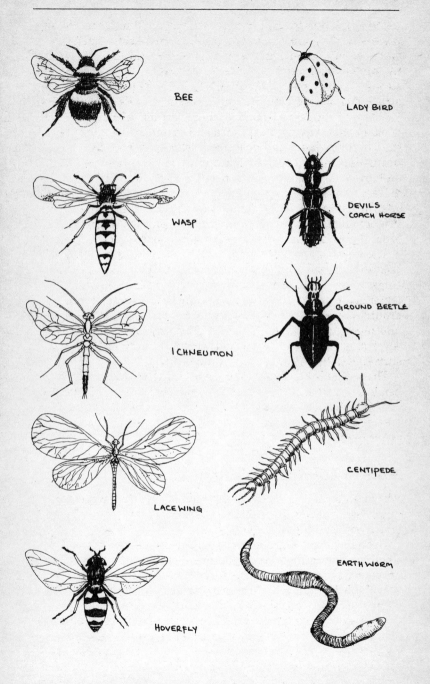

BEE

LADY BIRD

WASP

DEVILS COACH HORSE

ICHNEUMON

GROUND BEETLE

LACE WING

CENTIPEDE

HOVERFLY

EARTH WORM

larvae which are small, and green-grey or brown in colour, and have a pair of small pincers, are avid aphic eaters.

Lacewings are similar in appearance to small dragonflies, 2cm long. Their bodies are brown or green with almost transparent wings. The larvae have a flattish, yellowy-brown body with a pair of pincers. They eat aphids and other small insects.

Ichneumon fly adults are about 1.8cm long. Their bodies are often banded with yellow or red stripes. They eat greenfly, and their larvae live on the bodies of caterpillars.

Earthworms vary in size, colour and length. They improve soil fertility through aeration, drainage and the incorporation of humus.

Centipedes are fast moving and have one pair of legs per segment. They are red, brown or yellow in colour, larger and flatter than millipedes, up to 5cm long, and live in and on the soil eating small slugs, snails and insects.

Ground or carabid beetles are 2.5cm long, and dark metallic in colour. The larvae are dark brown and caterpillar-like with two whiskers on their tails. They ear insects, slugs, snails, mites and flies.

Devil's Coach Horse have similar larvae to the ground beetle. This beetle is black and about 2.5cm long. It runs rapidly and turns up its tail when it is disturbed. It eats soil insects.

PESTS

Aphids are very common small, soft, pear-shaped insects about 1–2mm long. They multiply profusely and live on the sap from plant leaves and stems.

Cutworms have fat, soil-coloured bodies up to 5cm long with sucker feet. They damage newly-planted cabbages, beetroots and carrots by eating through the stem at soil level. The moth larvae of several different species are known as cutworms.

Leatherjacket (crainfly larvae) are fat, soft and earthy in colour, up to 4cm long, legless, and have no distinct head. They eat roots and stems of many plants and attack above and below ground.

Millipedes have smooth round bodies with two legs per segment. They are slow-moving and curl up when disturbed. They eat bulbs, potatoes and many plant roots.

Wireworms (click beetle larvae) are about 2.5cm long. they

have three pairs of legs and a tough wire-like body which is golden yellow, and eat dead vegetation and potatoes, carrots and other vegetables. It is four to five years before the larvae develop into click beetles.

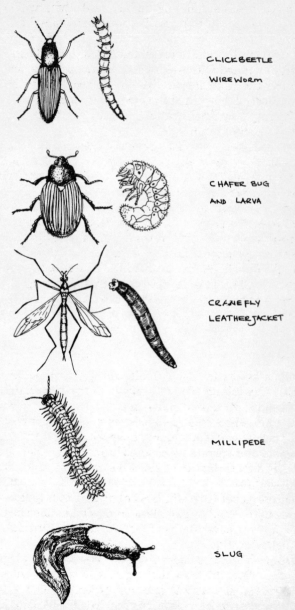

CLICK BEETLE
WIREWORM

CHAFER BUG
AND LARVA

CRANEFLY
LEATHERJACKET

MILLIPEDE

SLUG

Slugs are soft-bodied and slimy. There are several differently coloured species 2.5–5cm long. They eat dead vegetation and growing plants above and below ground.

Many vegetable diseases are caused by fungi, which attacks the roots and foilage of plants. Symptoms may be mishapen growth, moulds, mildew, or spots on the foilage, all of which can be avoided by good gardening practice. Viral diseases are more difficult to recognise – affects plants may be mishapen or grow out of character compared to others of the same variety. There are no cures for viral diseases: affected plants should be dug up and destroyed, and resistant varieties grown in the future.

CONTROL OF PESTS AND DISEASES

Some pests and diseases will have to be controlled using pesticides. Choose the weakest organically-based preparation that will be effective but will kill as few other insects as possible, and will cause the least pollution to the soil and plants. Although organic pesticides break down into harmless products fairly rapidly, they are posionous and should be treated with great care. Some of the safer pesticides can be made at home, and others bought from garden shops, or from the Henry Doubleday Research Association.

Pesticides

Product	Comments	Effective against
Bordeaux mixture	Ready-made mixture of copper sulphate and slaked lime. Mix with water and use immediately.	Potato Blight on potatoes and tomatoes; Peach Leaf Curl; Canker; reduces Rose Black Spot, Mildew and Rust.
Burgundy mixture	Ready-made brands or make using 85g copper sulphate dissolved in 4.5 litres of hot water. Leave to cool, add 110g of washing soda dissolved in a further 4.5 litres of water. Mix the two together. Homemade, it is very strong.	Safe as general fungicide and preventative spray for Potato Blight on tomatoes and potatoes. Use on a tree or bush fruit when it is leafless.
Comfrey	Liquid form (see page 48) to make it).	General preventative measure against attacks especially for Potato Blight and Chocolate Spot on beans.

Product	Comments	Effective against
Derris – extract of roots from several plants	Available as liquid or dust. Harmless to bees and hoverfly larvae. Harmful to fish and ladybird larvae and eggs and lacewing larvae. Should only be used if simple detergent solutions have failed. Derris remains toxic for 48 hours.	Liquid – Aphids, Red Spider Mite, Caterpillars. Dust – Flea Beetle.
Downy mildew mixture	Dissolve ½kg of washing soda and 250g of soft soap in 25 litres of cold water. Harmless.	American Gooseberry, Mildew and other downy mildews.
Fertosan slug killer	Powder made into a liquid. Keeps ground slugs and snails free for several months. Harmless to mammals, birds, earthworms. Do not apply in dry conditions.	Slugs and snails.
Nicotine	Available as 2 per cent liquid nicotine soap. Kills insect predators and bees – spray in the evening. Poisonous to mammals – wear gloves when using it. Do not eat plants for 48 hours after spraying	Caterpillars and aphids, Mealy Bugs, Pea and Bean Weevils, Red Spider Mite.
Powdery mildew mixture	Dissolves 5g potassium permanganate in 5 litres water. Harmless.	Pea Mildew and other mildews.
Pyrethrum	Available as liquid or dust. Harmless to bees and natural predators.	Aphids, Caterpillars, Flea Beetles, fungus.
Quassia – made from woodchips from Picrasma quassioides	Simmer 25g of woodchips (available from HDRA) in 1 litre water for 1 hour. Top up water to maintain level. Strain liquid and dilute 1:4 with water before use. Harmless to bees and ladybirds.	Small Caterpillars, Aphids, Leaf Miners and Sawflies.
Rhubarb, elder leaves, orange peel spray	Chop up 450g leaves or several orange skins and boil for ½ hour in 1.2 litres of water. Add more water to maintain level. Strain mixture and use. Harmless to bees, ladybirds and their larvae. Harmful to hoverfly larvae.	Aphids and small caterpillars. Vegetable fungicide.
Soap Spray (homemade)	Any soap can be used but industrial soft soap is best. Dissolve 55g soap in 4.5 litres of hot water. When cool spray on foilage. If the solution is too concentrated it may interfere with leaf respiration.	Blackfly, Greenfly, Mealy Bugs, Red Spider Mites and Whitefly. Deters Aphids if used in the early stages of attack.

FURTHER READING

Henry Doubleday Research Association booklets:
- *Vegetable Pest and Disease Control*
- *Feeding the Soil*
- *Raised Bed Gardening*
- *Potato Growing for Gardeners*
- *Comfrey for Gardeners and Smallholders*

Allan, Mea, *The Gardener's Book of Weeds,* Macdonalds and Jane's, 1978

Elphinstone, Margaret and Langley, Julia, *The Holistic Gardener,* Thorsons, 1987

Franck, Gertrud, *Companion Gardening: Successful Gardening the Organic Way,* Thorsons, 1983

Hay, Jim, *Vegetables Naturally,* Century, 1985

Mammond, J.L., and Mammond, Barbara, *The Village Labourer,* Longmans, 1911

HMSO *The Thorp Report: Report of the Departmental Committee of Inquiry into Allotments,* HMSO Command Paper No 4166, 1969

Hessayon, Dr D.G., *Be your own Vegetable Doctor,* Pan Britannica Industries Ltd, 1978

Hillman, Peter, *How Does Your Garden Grow?,* Croom Helm, 1985

Hills, Lawrence, *Fertility Gardening,* Cameron and Tayleur, 1981

Hills, Lawrence, *Organic Gardening,* Penguin, 1977

Hills, Lawrence, *Grow Your Own Fruit and Vegetables,* Faber and Faber, 1971

Larkcom, Joy, *Vegetables from Small Gardens,* Faber and Faber, 1976

Low, Sampson, *The Allotment Book: A visual guide to successful growing,* Sampson Low, 1977

McLaughlin, Eve and McLaughlin, Terence, *Cost-Effective Self-sufficiency or The Middle-Class Peasant,* David and Charles, 1978

Riley, Peter, *Economic Growth: The allotment campaign guide,* Friends of the Earth, 1979

Salter, P.J. *et al., Know and Grow Vegetables,* Vols 1 and 2, Oxford University Press, 1979

Seymour, John, *The Self-Sufficient Gardener,* Faber and Faber, 1978

Shewell-Cooper, Dr W.E., *Basic Book of Garden Pests and Diseases,* Barrie and Jenkis, 1978

Shewell-Cooper, Dr W.E., *Basic Book of Natural Gardening,* Barrie and Jenkins, 1978

Shewell-Cooper, Dr W.E., *The Complete Vegetable Grower,* Faber and Faber, 1973

USEFUL ADDRESSES

CHASE SEEDS LTD (organically grown seeds)
Gibraltar House
Shepperton
Middlesex TW17 8AQ

FRIENDS OF THE EARTH
26–28 Underwood Street
London N1 7JQ

HENRY DOUBLEDAY RESEARCH ASSOCIATION
National Centre for Organic Gardening
Ryton-on-Dunsmore
Coventry CV8 3LG

NATIONAL SOCIETY OF ALLOTMENT AND LEISURE
GARDENERS LTD
Hunters Road
Corby
Northants NN17 1JE

ROYAL HORTICULTURAL SOCIETY
Wisley
Woking
Surrey GU23 6QB

SOIL ASSOCIATION
86–88 Colston Street
Bristol BS1 5BB

ABOUT THE AUTHORS

ROB BULLOCK started his gardening career when he was two years old, by helping his father and grandfather run an organic allotment. In more recent years he has worked several allotments of his own, and now has the good fortune to have a large vegetable plot which he reclaimed from the wild six years ago (with the help of two Tamworth pigs!). He lives and works in Sheffield.

GILLIE GOULD has a degree in ecology. She has always been interested in environmental issues and has worked regularly with Conservation Volunteers and Working Weekends On Organic Farms. Since moving to Sheffield three years ago, she has run her own allotment where she grows vegetables organically.